No Ordinary Life

Lydia Lewis

This edition first published in paperback by
Michael Terence Publishing in 2024
www.mtp.agency

ISBN 9781800946965

Michael Terence
Publishing

1

My Journey Begins

My story begins a long, long time ago in 1961. I was born on Tuesday the 17th of October, a wet, rainy, windy, cool day in North Humberside. My mum gave birth to me at home, at that time my three brothers and I lived on an estate in the east part of Hull. Mum was so pleased to have a baby girl after having three boys.

My mum was called Mary and my dad, Charles. They had been married for 10 years at that time. I was the fourth child; my older brother was called Simon, and he was the eldest, then there was Darren and Tony was my youngest brother at just 4½ years old. He was very pleased to have a baby sister.

As I was born around 4 a.m. on the 17th of October, she wanted to have me at home. Mum had quite a long labour with me. She, like a lot of mothers, felt more comfortable with a home birth as that way she was able to move about and walk around. The midwife was there with Mum at the time of my birth. However, there were two of us. Mum had twins, like me a little girl, though sadly she died due to the fact that I was a big baby weighing 8lb 8oz, the other baby did not have enough room to survive. I did not realise then but boy did I need those extra pounds as to what was to come. This was a very sad time for my mum, having lost one baby; this was all hushed up by the doctor and midwife.

Mum asked to see me, to see if I had all my limbs as around that time, a lot of babies were being born with thalidomide. Yes, all my limbs were there, and Mum was very happy as she was desperate to have a baby girl. Within an hour of my birth, I was introduced to my youngest brother, Tony, who took a quick look at me and said, "Awe a baby sister!" then ran away to play.

A few hours later that day, evening time it was, I started to go blue, so Mum wrapped me in a warm blanket. She held me close for hours. Every time she returned me to my cot, I turned blue. She became very anxious and worried. Around an hour later, Mum's neighbour called to see her. Mum told her about me. She said that I did not look good at all, so Mum asked if she could use her phone to call for an ambulance as something was seriously wrong with me. The ambulance arrived within 15 minutes, with two paramedics; one asked Mum where the father was, and she told her that my dad had fallen asleep drunk like he usually was. They were not happy about his behaviour at all. Mum's neighbour looked after my brothers whilst Mum and I were rushed to a little cottage hospital around 2 miles from our home. I was admitted straight away, seen by various doctors, also a paediatrician, who took one look at me and advised Mum to call for a priest, as there was no way that I would survive the night. The hospital staff did various tests on me, they found that I had huge cysts on both my lungs which were filled with fluid and they both needed to be drained. It would be a massive operation with a general anaesthetic, a huge thing for a newborn baby to undergo.

However, my mum consented to it. The paediatrician who operated had quite big hands and the procedure took around two to three hours, during which time my heart stopped four times and I died, but fortunately for me, I was resuscitated. During all this time, my mum was in the hospital chapel, praying for me to live. Mum was a very religious person and believed that I would survive, which I did, much to her relief. Through all the worry, anxiety and stress over me, Mum had to deal with this on her own, she was very positive that her little girl was a fighter and would survive. She had no support from anyone at the time, my dad was drunk and useless so he did not know what had happened to me. Her precious little girl did pull through. By this time the priest had arrived, and Mum told him that she would like to call me Lydia, which she did. She stayed at the hospital with me for the next two days.

After my operation, I was placed in an incubator. The paediatrician came to see me and he told Mum that the operation had gone well, and all the cysts had been removed, though it could take a little while for me to recover from such a massive operation for one so young and fragile. He stated that I might be left with a heart murmur, but not to worry as most people can live with this all their lives with no trouble from it at all. He advised Mum to go home and get some much-needed rest as she had had no sleep for two days. She arrived home around 9 a.m. She was very tired but wanted to see my brothers who were being looked after by our next-door neighbour. She had fed them and got them ready for school.

Mum decided to walk home from the hospital. Well, she had no money for a bus. We were poor. My dad did not have a car, he was an electrician and cycled to work every day. As Mum approached our house, Dad was on his way to work. He said, "Where have you been all this time? Also, where's the bairn?"

To which Mum replied, "As you were out of it, drunk at the time, our baby girl Lydia had to be admitted to hospital, she needed an emergency operation, she nearly died, that's where I've been, with our daughter. Did you get the boys off to school? Or did Edna from next door?"

Dad did not reply as he had left for work. That day, Mum really tried to get some sleep but it was no use, she was just so worried about me. She had just gone downstairs when Edna knocked on the door. Mum shouted, "It's open!" She came in and made Mum a cup of tea. As she did so, Mum said,

"Thank you for getting the ambulance for me, it was good of you to let me use your 'phone, also thank you for looking after the boys, hope they behaved themselves while I was at the hospital. I'm heading up there myself soon to check on Lydia."

Edna said to Mum, "You look so tired, I bet that you have come straight home, not having anything to eat. You need to eat, love, to keep your strength up as that sweet bairn needs you. Let me make you something; perhaps poached egg on toast?"

Mum said, "I don't think that I can stomach anything as I'm so worried about her, Edna. I nearly lost my lovely precious little girl you know, she is stable for now in an incubator. When I go to see her, I have to wear all this protective gear, a gown, gloves and the like, so I don't take any infections into the room which she will pick up. Look, Edna, I have knitted her this lovely brown teddy bear!" In time, this was to become my favourite soft toy, though most times I would throw it out of my cot.

"It's lovely!" said Edna. "What name did you choose for the bairn?"

"Lydia," Mum replied. "Lydia is a good name for her though I do not think that Charles will agree with me. Oh! Edna, I so wanted a girl, this is what I prayed for every day I was pregnant," said Mum thoughtfully. "The doctor asked me where was Lydia's father. I was just too embarrassed to tell him the truth so I just said at work."

As the days went by, Mum came to see me every day, sometimes staying at the hospital for hours on end. She did not want to leave me; she would just look at me. If she wanted to give me anything, she had to put on all the protective clothing for fear of any kind of infection. Sometimes Dad would visit me, when he could find the time of course, or when he was not in the pub. I was monitored by a nurse every hour, checked over by the duty doctor, and now and again the paediatrician would call in to see how I was doing and if I was improving.

Mum made friends at the hospital with a lady who had just given birth to a baby boy around the same time as me. Like me, her baby was poorly but not placed in an incubator. He had cystic fibrosis. At that time, they did not have the proper medicines to help this illness, like we do today, and sadly for her, he died. Unfortunately, there was nothing that the doctors could do for her baby boy. So Mum supported her through this very sad time. They became best friends and she became my godmother. Mum was very sad for her friend who became very depressed over her loss and her husband, not being able to cope with the loss of his son, unfortunately had a full nervous breakdown. He had to be hospitalized and given various treatments, including electric shock therapy for his breakdown. Afterwards, he could not remember being in hospital or his treatment.

As the weeks went by, I became much stronger. I was fed by a tube so all of Mum's milk had to be thrown away as she was unable to breastfeed me. Mum would show me the teddy outside the incubator, she would gently talk to me and read me some nice baby stories. For hours on end each day, she would be there willing me to get better; she desperately needed to give me a cuddle and to hold me.

As the weeks turned into months, Mum could be found at the hospital chapel praying for me, caring, supporting me and at the same time looking after my 3 brothers who kept asking her, "When's baby Lydia coming home?" To which Mum would reply, "When you see all the tiny little buds shooting up in the springtime, that's when. So, we will all just have to be patient and wait, won't we?"

Mum and Dad's marriage was on shaky ground. Back then, mainly due to the demon drink which he could not resist, this, Dad's problem, tainted their marriage right from the start. Mum did not drink; she disliked the atmosphere in pubs, the noise and just about everything whereas Dad was right at home there. I sometimes think that he loved the drink even more than his family. When they had been married for nearly 11 years, Mum had had enough of all his drinking, coming home late, spending all of our money on drink, leaving her with barely anything for housekeeping, food etc, and it was us kiddies and Mum who were going without the basics. Dad never had any money so we all suffered. It was no life for Mum, we had nothing, Dad had drunk it all. Sometimes he would spend the rent money, sometimes the food money, the times that he had lost his job due to not turning up for work, being in the pub.

Dad had been promoted to foreman in his electrician job which was a lot better paid, but once again he lost that job due to his drinking problem. Our home was very clean, though we only had rugs on the floor as Mum could not afford carpets. She kept the place spotless; she cooked, and she cleaned for us all, not once complaining. Mum was a brilliant cook, a very good housewife, and a loving, caring kind, wonderful mother. The only problem was that she was married to Dad. So, somewhere at this point in Mum's life, she made the decision to end their marriage. She was very, very unhappy and felt that she could not live like this anymore, so decided to apply for a divorce.

The following week she consulted a solicitor who started divorce proceedings for her, this was around the time I was 8 months old. Their marriage was going nowhere. Mum felt that in time Dad would bring her, me and my 3 brothers down to his level. Mum had nothing. It would be best all around if they just parted with Mum having full custody of us children. From the day I was born, right until now, I never felt loved or wanted by my dad, I do not know why as I never got to know him. Later on in my life, that was my choice though. I really did not want anything to do with him due to the awful way he had treated my mum, me and my 3 brothers. I always knew that Mum loved me, she showed it in many ways.

When I was around 18 months old, my parents divorced. My 3 brothers and I stayed with Mum; she was given full custody. It was just as well as my dad was not responsible to look after us, especially me, as I required round-the-clock care and attention. Their divorce came through at the end of March. By that time, Dad had already moved out, and gone to live with his parents. So began the next chapter of my life.

2

Being a poorly baby, I required a lot of attention throughout the day, so my oldest brother Simon took care of his brothers whilst Mum was busy with me. This was a very difficult time for Mum as I was unable to breastfeed from her, so her milk had to be thrown away. She would make a mix of formula up for me, however being so ill, I did not feel like eating or drinking and most times after Mum had fed me, unfortunately, I brought it all back up. I was unable to digest it. This was most upsetting for her though she did have a lot of patience with me; it is just as well she did. Sometimes, it would take her 3-4 hours, just to feed me, for me to keep it down.

Looking back on my life, I really do not know how Mum managed to look after us all and put bread on the table. We always had a good meal every day. Mum became like a mother and father figure to us all, she did everything for us, never, ever complaining. From the age of 6 months, I had to regularly attend hospital appointments for check-ups. Around the time I was 11 months old, Mum became very worried about my limbs, so she took me to see our family doctor for advice. I did not move my arms or legs and they were quite floppy. The doctor examined me and told Mum that he would refer me to see a paediatrician as soon as possible. There was definitely a problem with me as I was not developing as an 11-month-old baby should do.

A few weeks later, found Mum and me at the hospital with me being examined by not one paediatrician, but two. After this, he asked one of his other colleagues for a second opinion on what could be my problem; what was the cause of my floppy, lifeless limbs, legs and arms. After much consulting between themselves, they came to the same conclusion, that I was suffering from muscular dystrophy, which was quite unusual in a girl, it was mainly seen in boys. But all the signs they said led them to believe that this was the case with me. They informed Mum that as I got older, it would get worse and I could end up in a wheelchair in time, not being able to ever walk on my own. This was their diagnosis, my future looked very bleak indeed.

My mum was in shock at this news, she was so upset not able to process this and take it all in. When we left the hospital, she was in tears, most distressed and worried about me. We went straight home and as we arrived, Edna from next door was just about to knock on our door. Well, she took one look at Mum and said,

"I think what you need right now is a nice cup of tea. I will take Lydia and hold her for a while. You look done in, love, what's happened?"

So, after Edna made a cup of tea, she held me in her arms whilst Mum explained what the doctors had told her at the hospital. Like Mum, Edna too was most upset, she could not believe my diagnosis. Mum said that she felt all the doctors were wrong. They wanted to visit Mum and Dad at home to discuss this further and what would happen to me later in life, and also if there were any questions that Mum and Dad would like answered. So, Mum had to contact Dad who was living with his parents, and tell him that the doctors would like to speak to them both. My diagnosis apparently was most baffling to them, in view of the fact that I had 3 healthy, strong brothers, why was I the one with muscular dystrophy? Dad said that he would like to attend this meeting, which would be in two weeks at our home in the evening.

The 3 paediatricians arrived, tea was offered to them and so began the discussion. Questions were asked like if my parents were related. Was there anyone in the family who had had muscular dystrophy? Did my brothers have the same father as me? The discussion went on right until the early hours of the morning and the doctors left our home more confused than ever, there was just no explanation for it all. Mum and Dad were mentally exhausted by this time; Mum felt that she was no further ahead, however, she did not believe that I would never walk. She knew that one day I would walk, and she was very confident about this, as she said to herself, "I will show them, that they are wrong, my precious little girl will walk, she will walk to her mummy."

After that, Mum started my treatment every single day. She would massage olive oil into my lifeless limbs, day after day, week after week. She persevered with this routine, and she never, ever, gave up on me, she really believed in me and that in time I would walk. Around this time, I was about 2½ years old, we had an appointment with my paediatrician, the one who had operated on me when I was one day old. We arrived at the hospital and Mum was very confident that I would be able to show the doctor just what I could do.

The paediatrician examined me, checking me over, he turned to Mum and said, "I believe that you have something to show me?"

To which Mum replied, "No, not me, Lydia has, just watch her."

Mum took me off her knee and set me down on the soft carpeted floor of the consulting room. She said softly, "Lydia, come walk to Mummy, show this nice man what you can do."

Well, I stood up, I was a little wobbly for my first few steps but then I got in my stride. Mum held out her hands to me as I walked right across the floor to her.

"Good girl!" she said. "Good girl, mummy knew that you could do it!"

The doctor was absolutely stunned and speechless as to what he had just seen, so he called for one of his colleagues to come in. It was the same one who had visited Mum and Dad at home. He too was amazed and said to Mum,

"It is like a miracle, how is this possible?"

The paediatrician turned and said, "This is all down to you, Mrs Lewis, your determination and perseverance has paid off. I congratulate you for all you have done for your daughter. As Lydia is still so young, I feel that we need to make some support for her legs and ankles to strengthen them, something she can wear every day, and take them off at nighttime to sleep. So, I would be grateful if you and Lydia could come to see me next week, so Lydia can be measured up for some little protective ankle boots, made to fit, which she will have to wear for the next 3 to 4 years and we will review her every 6 months to see how she is coping with them."

The bobby boots as I called them were to strengthen my ankles and legs. It took me a while to get used to them. Mum took them off me before I went to bed.

In time, I became a very picky, slow eater and it would take me a long time to eat my food. Whilst my 3 brothers were fast easters, sometimes they had to wait for me to finish, especially if we were having a pudding. I do not feel that they liked meal time with me. About 6 months later, my dad started pestering Mum saying that he would like to see the boys. He came around to our house at night and made himself a nuisance, ringing the doorbell, and banging on the door. Sometimes he was so drunk he would fall asleep in our shed. Mum went to see a solicitor to get a court order, to keep him away, which it did.

It was peaceful in our home for a few years, after Dad had stopped bothering us. As I grew older, though still petite and thin for my age, the boots had to be replaced with a bigger size. Mum took me on the bus to the hospital.

My two older brothers, Simon and Darren would fight constantly, and pick fights with our neighbours' children; all 3 of them were really a handful for my mum. She obviously had to chastise them which she did, sometimes they really played her up. Looking back, it must have been hard for her with me being poorly too. I cannot remember Simon and Darren ever playing with me; the youngest one, Tony, would sometimes come to my pram and tickle me, which I did not like.

By this time, I was around 3½ years old, I was a very sad, scowly little girl, sadly not very close to Mummy or any of my brothers. I guess I felt a lot of bitterness and anger which showed on my face and made me most unpleasant to everyone. Perhaps this was one of the reasons that my brothers would not play with me, they did not want my company. I really disliked having my photograph taken, when Mum was taking it, I would stick my tongue out and scowl at her.

Around this time, Mum became very friendly with Edna's husband, Frank, whom Mum had hardly ever seen as all he ever did was work and work. He worked various shifts, sometimes in the day, and sometimes in the night. As Edna was a few years older than Frank, she had various health problems and did not like to go out much. She loved her home more, she did not like to go to clubs, pubs etc. She felt that Frank should have an outlet on a night when he was not working, so she suggested that as Mum and she were very good friends, Mum needed a break away from the home and children, especially the children.

She said to Mum, "Why don't you let my Frank take you out one evening, perhaps to the pub? You know all he ever does is work. All you seem to do is look after those bairns of yours and keep house. Don't you ever feel lonely and want some adult company sometimes? Oh, go on Mary," she said, "It will do you the world of good to get out for a few hours at least. Don't worry about the bairns, I will take good care of them. You just let Frank take you out and enjoy the evening."

Well, Mum hesitated at first, then she said, "Oh, it is so good of you Edna to think of me, as long as you don't mind. I have been feeling a bit lonely recently, it would be so good to have some adult company. It has been a very long time since I last went out, I do hope that I will not be too boring for Frank."

The very next evening, Frank came calling for Mum. He was used to our house, as Mum sometimes asked Edna if Frank could do some DIY jobs around our home. Mum was looking very nice, off they both went, just to the local pub down the road as Mum did not want to be too far from home. When she did return home, the very first thing she always did when she had been out was to come and check on us all, to see if we were all okay. We were fast asleep as usual.

Mum went out with Frank a few more times after that. She rather liked his company, the fact that he was an honest working family man, having 2 children himself. Then for some reason, Mum stopped seeing him. She looked worried, anxious and sad most days.

3

A New Addition To The Family

Edna came to see Mum, as she usually did every day. Mum had something to tell her, though she did not know just how she could find the words to say it. She really did struggle to tell Edna as she felt if she did, it would definitely be the end of their friendship. After a few minutes, Mum finally had the courage to say it,

"I'm pregnant Mary. I am so sorry, but it's Frank's baby. We only made love once, please forgive me as I have wronged you, I'm so very, very sorry."

To which Edna replied, "I guessed that there was something wrong with you not seeing Frank anymore. You have not told him yet, have you?"

"No," Mum answered. "How can I tell him? You are his wife, he has 2 children already, this was not meant to happen. Oh Edna, what am I going to do?" Mum was crying at this point, she said, "I have betrayed your trust, Edna, and ruined our friendship at the same time. It is all my fault, I do wish that I had never gone out with Frank to start with as I did not feel comfortable about the arrangement and told him so on many occasions, to me it did not feel right."

To this, Edna replied, raising her voice, "Oh, you silly woman, it's my fault, all my fault, no-one else's, do not blame yourself, lass. I thought that I was helping the both of you, who could have known that this would happen?"

"So," said Mum, wiping her tears away, "You don't blame me?"

"No," she replied. "It takes two to tango. He is more to blame, so I feel it would be best for all if you told him about the baby, Mary, as soon as possible."

That evening, when Frank came home from work around 8 p.m., Mum went to see him to tell him her news. He was not pleased at all, he was angry, and said, "We only made love once, that night when your lights went out, do you remember?"

"I remember it well. Do you really think I want another baby? I already have 4 children, one poorly child too, oh you selfish man! Tell me Frank, what am I going to do? You have a wife and 2 children; will you divorce Edna for me? I don't think so. Anyway, I will make it easy for you, I'm having this baby, you will stay with Edna and continue to be a good father to your children, look after them, also Edna, they need you more than me."

"Have you really considered this, Mary?" he said. "It's a huge decision to make on your own."

"Yes," she answered. "Let this be the last word said on this mistake we have both made, only I will have to live with it for the rest of my life."

She turned and walked away from Frank, Edna and their friendship. They never spoke about it again.

Edna did not come to our house much after that. Five months went by, Mum had to go to the hospital, she was there for a few days to keep a check on the baby as it was near her time. Mum's friend came to visit her whilst there. Then the next thing we all knew, Mum had had the baby, a baby girl and she called her Mandy. She was a chubby little baby with lots of dark hair, just like Mum's.

A few weeks later, Mum was admitted to hospital for treatment of some kind, she was there for a very, very long time. My brothers went to stay with Mum's best friend, whilst Edna kindly offered to look after me and Mandy. The months went by and winter was on the way before Mum eventually came home to us. She seemed different somehow. All the boys were pleased to see her, I was too. Mandy missed Mum, she was around six months old and even chubbier. Looking back, it must have been very difficult for Mum, as well as all my brothers, as the oldest two were aware of the situation, though they never mentioned it to Mum.

One day whilst we were all having tea, Mum said, "I have decided that we will be moving to another area, as we cannot stay here. I am sure that you will all like it there as it is a house, it has a big garden, there is a school nearby, shops too, it is a lovely big house. So, boys, I will need some boxes and newspaper to wrap things up in. Do you think that you will be able to help me with this? It is quite exciting; don't you think boys?"

The winter arrived with deep blankets of snow on the ground. Mum packed and wrapped what little goods we had and two weeks later we moved onto a nice estate in a friendly, though nosey area. Mandy was not very old when we moved into our new house, it was an extremely cold day, my brothers were moving small things into the house, one at a time in fact. Mum was busy trying to light the fire; the neighbour from next door, well the nets were twitching. A little after we had all moved our things into our new house, she came to ask Mum for something. I think it was so she could get a good look at us, and see how many we were.

To get to our house, you had to go down a very long, narrow path, the house was at the end and as I looked out the back window, I could see that we had a huge garden and I mean huge. Me and Mandy were to share a bedroom as were my 3 brothers. The house had 3 bedrooms, the lounge was really big, and so was the kitchen.

As I was around 4½ years old by this time, I had an appointment to see the paediatrician again at the hospital for a check-up, so Mum asked Grandma, my dad's mother if she could look after Mandy whilst we went. My brothers had gone to their new school, which was just down the road, a short walk away for them. Once again, we caught the bus to the hospital and I was shown into a room with Mum. Two doctors came along with my paediatrician, who examined me. The doctors were junior ones, learning, and they listened to what the doctor had to say. He asked Mum if I had been enrolled at a nursery or a school. He suggested that I should go to a specialist school, not a mainstream one, due to all my health issues at that time. I was still wearing my little booties, which I had got used to. He felt that I would do better at a special school and not be held back with my learning and education.

Mum stood up facing him, and said angrily, "No, my daughter will go to an ordinary school, she will do well there, no way will I be sending her to a special school, she does not need it, I will enrol her into a nursery first to see how she gets on."

"Well perhaps you are right," he said, "after all mothers know best, and she is a credit to you already. I would like to see Lydia in one year so that we can check her height, weight and so on as she is rather small and slim for her age. Is she still struggling with her food?"

"She likes to eat a little and often," replied Mum, "though she is still very slow at eating, and very picky with her food. I expect that as she grows up, this will improve in time, I do hope so."

Mum shook my doctor's hand as we left. When we arrived home, Grandma was there and Mum put the kettle on for a cup of tea. Mandy was asleep in her cot and I went up to my bedroom to play with one of my toys. Then, before I knew it, my brothers had returned from school asking,

"What's for tea, Mum?"

"What's your new school like? Did you enjoy your first day there?"

"It's alright," he replied. "Can we go out to play now, just for a little while until tea?"

"Yes, okay, just Darren and Tony though as I would like Simon to go to the shops for me, we are out of bread. If he does not get it there will be no tea for any of us. You be good boys now; don't get up to any mischief and don't go too far away from home."

Before you knew it, they were gone, running down the street without a care in the world. The winter was especially cruel that year, though it always was in the north, the snow came thick and fast.

Then, at last, spring was on the way. Mum had not managed to plant anything as she had been too busy with the move, looking after me and Mandy and organizing the house. Mum could not afford carpets on the floor so we just had rugs, though our home was always clean, tidy and neat; she made sure it was kept that way.

One evening we all sat down to our dinner around a big table in the kitchen; we were having fish. My brothers just loved their food as they quickly ate theirs while I just picked at mine. I did not like all the little bones in the fish, so I did not eat it. Mum noticed this and spent the next hour or so deboning the fish for me. By this time, Mandy and my brothers had eaten theirs, though Mum always gave us most of the fish whilst she often went without food herself, to feed us and give us the best. When the fish was deboned, I really enjoyed it. I guess you could say that I was a fussy eater, not like now; I eat most things and have a good appetite. After this, my brothers told Mum that I was too picky and that she should just leave the fish as it was, I would eat it when I was hungry. Mum always helped me with my meals, never getting cross or annoyed; she really did have a lot of patience with me.

Mum liked the springtime; she knitted all our jumpers, hats, gloves, scarves etc. She would always dress me and Mandy in the same outfits. We would go to the park, Mum pushing Mandy in her pram, me walking by her side, always with my little booties on. I enjoyed the park, I would go on the swing, Mum gently pushing me back and forth. The springtime in those days was always pleasant, nice and sunny, not too hot which was perfect. One day Mum suggested that both me and Mandy should have some photographs taken. I was not keen on having my photo taken at the best of times. Mum took some good photographs of the 3 boys together, then she said that a nice photo of me and Mandy was called for. Well, I tried my best to get away from her, I tried to hide but she just found me.

"Come on Lydia," she said. "We must have one of you and Mandy for the photo album."

She carefully placed Mandy on a blanket on the ground, I was to sit right next to Mandy and have a big smile on my face which I did not. I would not smile as usual, I was scowling away, pulling a face as I did so. I really hated my photo being taken, even today I do not like it. Mum picked some daisies from the garden and gave them to me to hold, which was nice, so I was okay with them. Mandy had a little toy on the blanket while Mum clicked away. Oh boy, was I pleased when it was over!

4

Off to School

I was a very shy, introverted little girl who had no confidence whatsoever. Mandy, my sister was the complete opposite. Perhaps that's why we never got along, I do not know, looking back I guess that I was a difficult person to understand and get on with. The photographs that came back were very good, especially of the boys. My photo with Mandy was okay, though like always, I was not smiling. Mandy was lovely and cute. No one took a photo of Mum that day. Mandy was around ten months at the time and she was crawling. However, later on, she tried to stand up. When she was around 14 months old, she would hold onto things and try to walk, at which point I would naughtily push her back down. This happened most days and Mum would always tell me off for doing so. Perhaps in my own way, I was jealous of Mandy. I do not know; it was not a nice thing for me to do. Sometimes, Simon would shout at me to stop me from doing it, but I still continued. As the year went by, Mandy continued to grow and become stronger. She could now walk on her own and Mum would take us all and my brothers to the park; she could never afford to take us to the seaside.

September was fast approaching which meant that I would be going to a mainstream school. I was very anxious and apprehensive about it, I felt quite scared, having always been at home with Mum and my siblings. On my first day at school, Mum came with me and stayed a while so I could get used to it. After she left, I cried and cried, I felt so frightened and scared, I did not like this feeling. The day went well, though was I glad when Mum came to collect me and we walked home. The boys were out, and they returned a little later, then Mum asked them to go tidy their bedroom. I guess being boys it had become untidy.

At that time, I had my bedroom all to myself as Mandy was in Mum's bedroom so she could keep an eye on her if she wanted a feed. She did not seem to cry a lot, she was around 15 months old now, still very chubby, but unlike me, she loved her food. The boys came down wanting to go out and play. Mum said to them,

"Have you cleaned your room, as I asked you to?"

"Yes," they replied. "Can we go out now?"

Then they were gone; up to some mischief no doubt. Mum went up to check on the bedroom which was at the back of the house, with a good view of our garden. Then she started tea; we usually had it at the same time every night. Just as she was about to serve it, there was a knock on the front door.

"Simon, can you get that?" said Mum, "and tell them we are just about to have tea. Oh, who is it?"

Our neighbour from next door stood in the hall. She often came round either to borrow something or some money from Mum until she got paid; as she worked, I do not know what she spent all her money on. Mum would always lend her some, just to tide her over until pay day, though unlike Mum she was not a single mother with 5 mouths to feed. We were living on benefits because our father refused to pay Mum any maintenance money for me and my three brothers. However, Mandy's dad paid for her regularly.

Anyway, when Mum came back, she seemed quite annoyed, very rare for her, as with us she was always calm, caring and patient, also with most people. That night for tea, we were having fish again. The boys were tucking into theirs, Mandy was being fed by Mum and I was pulling the fish around on my plate when Simon piped up,

"Lydia, if you do not want your tea, I will have it. You are always the same whenever we have fish. I don't see why all of us have to wait for you to finish before we get our pudding!"

They wanted their tea there and then, not very patient at all, but looking back I suppose that I must have annoyed them sometimes with my strange eating habits. After Simon had told me off, I did not feel like my tea then, so I ate all the vegetables and just left the fish. Mum just gave me a look but did not say anything about me leaving it.

I soon got used to going to school, though I did not like the school meals. We were given a little bottle of fresh milk every day which was nice. I did not make any friends there as I was a rather shy and introverted child growing up. I never ever felt very happy or confident in myself. I guess that you could call me a very sad little girl, though Mum did indulge me and gave me a lot of attention, love and care. I would say that she really spoilt me, so much so, that in time to come this would cause my brothers a lot of grief as jealousy reared its head on many an occasion. I never really bonded with my sister, Mandy, and with my brothers never having any time for me, I was a loner. I did not mind my own company, often I would play alone with my toys, baby doll, teddies, pram etc.

Mum at that time was still not socializing. She spent most days cooking, cleaning, shopping, looking after us all, and keeping us all together as a family. She never seemed to have any time for herself. On an evening she could be found knitting some item of clothing for us. She was a very sociable, confident person who easily made friends. Her friend whom she met at the hospital would sometimes come to visit. Mandy's father did not have any contact with her at this time, this is the way that Mum wanted it, though he would always pay maintenance for her, and on time. Unlike my Dad, because Mum would have to go to the court collecting office practically every week to ask if there was any money for us, it was usually the same answer every time. But Mum always made sure that we children never went without. On our birthdays, she always managed to get us a nice present, also, at Christmas when we did celebrate it, we might have been lacking in money, but Mum more than made up for that, as we all had plenty of love, care and attention from her. She was a very good mother, she would stick up for us and she protected us in every way possible. Christmas was on the horizon by this time so once again, Mum started knitting for a company that would pay her for the items she made, then from that she would save up for Christmas to buy us some presents.

As we were approaching my sixth birthday, the days were becoming cooler, Mum would knit me some gloves, a hat and a nice scarf to match. All of my brothers had the same. Mum would knit all their jumpers in the same colour to match and we always looked smart and tidy going to school. Mum was even praised for it, which was very nice for her. My birthday came and went; Mum would have liked to take some photos of me, though she knew that I did not like this, so the camera was not brought out. The nights began to draw in, the days became shorter and it began to get colder with a bitter wind. I would walk to school each day, then Mum would collect me later on. I never liked the winter time, with all the snow and ice around.

Simon's 16th birthday was a few days after mine, which meant that he would soon be leaving school, hopefully finding a job as in the 1960s jobs were more accessible. A week or two after his birthday, Mum told us all that Simon would be leaving home and going to live with our grandparents, who were about 5 miles away. I never really knew them, not like Simon did, being the eldest, so he would remember them more. Mum had packed all Simon's clothes in a small case which she placed in the hall. That very same night harsh words and shouting could be heard coming from the living room; it must have been Simon and Mum; perhaps he did not want to leave.

I really did not know at the time Mum's reason for not wanting him to live with us anymore, though I do think Darren knew as he and Simon were very close, however sometimes they would flight like cat and dog. So, I guess that Darren would miss his big brother. I do know that Tony would be glad he was leaving us as one time Simon lashed out at him for something he had done and Tony had never got over it. Siblings do fight and squabble sometimes, perhaps over a favourite toy, but usually, they would kiss and make up. Everything would be alright then. Simon left that night; he said his goodbyes to everyone then he was gone.

So, Darren now became the head over us children. He was very popular at school, though he could be very naughty too. He used to love to bake, especially pies and cakes. Mum did not mind him baking as he always helped her with the chores, cleaning, tidying and cooking. He could do most things. He was a really good help to Mum, they were very close. However, what I did not realise then was that Simon and Darren both had issues. Simon was a bully from a young age. Darren had various issues, most of them occurring when he was at school. Sometimes Mum would have to see the headmaster of the school to get his problems sorted out. All this pressure, worry and stress she had to bear all on her own must have caused her a lot of sleepless nights. In a way it was not really right as she had enough to cope with on a daily basis, with me not being well, Mandy still so young and Tony to care for, though Tony never caused Mum and inch of trouble. Sometimes he was so quiet that we did not know if he was in or outside playing with his friends. Tony was a good boy.

All my brothers had different personalities, though Simon was the boss, he often let them know it too. I do believe that Darren and Tony were frightened of Simon, I know I was. I did not really miss my brothers as neither of them had much to do with me. I certainly would not miss Simon, though Darren would, as would Mum in her own way.

By the time Christmas was fast approaching, once again it would be a very hard time for Mum, trying to make ends meet and to be able to afford us all a present each. It would be our first Christmas in 16 years that we did not celebrate it with Simon. I guess he would be well fed and looked after by Grandma and Grandad, perhaps he may have found a job, so he could help them out with housekeeping money, board and such.

Mum managed to buy us all a nice gift and she made us a Christmas cake which was very tasty. We had jam tarts, mince pies and a lovely main meal, though not a turkey as it was too expensive for her, so we had pork and stuffing, along with vegetables, and after that, we had our delicious pudding. Darren would then start washing and drying all the pots, so this would enable Mum to have a sit-down, a relaxing time for her. She would make the most of our gifts in a way they were more personal in those days. We never had a television, Mum could just not afford one, so we would make our own entertainment by playing games such as Monopoly, Scrabble, cards, and Tiddlywinks, which me and Tony really liked; he was very good at it too. The Christmas holidays were always too long, I thought, I much preferred the new year. The new year, though very cold, snow and ice came and went and I went back to school again, as did the boys.

I loved the springtime, I still do now, it is one of the better seasons of the year. It was Darren's birthday at the end of the month so Mum would be worrying as to what she could afford to buy him. A few days after Darren's birthday, Tony came in from playing outside with his friends, he went running up to Mum and said,

"I have just seen our Darren with a suitcase; is he going somewhere, Mum?"

Mum looking hurt replied, "No not as far as I know. Where and when did you see him?"

"Just a few minutes ago" answered Tony.

Well, Mum ran to the lounge window. Peering out she could just make out a child's head bobbing up and down in the far distance. With tears in her eyes, she said to Tony,

"Another one of your brothers has left us. I guess it will be your turn next?"

Tony looked very upset at that remark, but he ran up to Mum and gave her a big hug as if to say, "No, not me Mum."

So that just left the four of us. After this, Mum seemed totally lost, in a daze, I thought at the time, just what is going on here? Why is everyone running away? Just what are they running from? Surely it can't be Mum as she is a wonderful, loving, caring, kind mother. Perhaps it was me as I was still not well, still having to have check-ups at the hospital once a year, still wearing those black, bulky ankle boots!

5

Then There Were Four

It was many years later when I became an adult that I found out the real reason why my two brothers left us and the family home. As you can imagine, Mum was very upset that Darren had gone. Now there were three children left and with Tony being the oldest, he had the responsibility of looking after us two girls. Being ten years old, he was not keen on this, though, at the end of the year, he would be going to another school for older children. Tony was always a quiet, thoughtful lad and nearly always did what he was told by Mum, it was only when he got with his older brothers that he would do silly things, following them around just like a little lost sheep.

By this time, Easter had come and gone. Mum always brought us an Easter egg. Grandma would come to see us and bring each of us one too. When the older boys were at home, and they reached the age of twelve, Mum would give them a choice to either have a bar of chocolate or go to the cinema. Most times they preferred going to the cinema as in those days you got two films for the price of one. Not like today, it is so expensive for a family to go to the cinema, the films always seem very short with no trailers or anything. Years ago, it was a real treat to go to the cinema, one we all used to look forward to. The month of May was now upon us, this was and still is my favourite month, all the colourful flowers were out, the birds were singing merrily in the trees and the days were longer, not too hot, just right.

Mum used to take us to the park; we were always very smart wearing our hand-knitted clothes and she was a very good knitter. I would go on the swing, though not too high, Mum would be watching me, she was very protective of all of us, especially me, in case I had a fall or an accident of any kind. Tony would run around, go on the roundabout, down the slide, Mandy was still too young to go on all the rides at the park.

Mum had managed to go dancing at a club. When the two older boys were at home, she had met a very nice gentleman there who, like her, loved dancing. He would sometimes call round to our house to see Mum, that way she did have some adult company which was nice for her. Simon never came to visit us after leaving home. I guess that he was busy trying to find a suitable job, he was never really mentioned to us by Mum.

That year, the summer was not too hot, so we were able to go and play in the park a lot, and also outside. Tony and his friends would play marbles. The game would last for ages; he collected various marbles and exchanged them with some of his friends. I liked playing hopscotch, skipping and marbles too, though sometimes I would cheat with marbles. Mum would sit on our doorstep to do some of her knitting, and the next-door neighbour sometimes would join Mum and have a natter at the same time. Our street was a quiet one with families with children and most times we all got on with each other. There were not many pets there, I suppose it was because they could not afford to keep a pet. Our next-door neighbour had a baby one year after Mandy. She would bring him outside in his pram in the summertime, all he did most of the time was cry, cry, cry with no let-up. Mum would often ask her why he was like that, did he want something?

Yet Mandy seemed to be content in her pram only crying for a feed, or her nappy changed. It was at this time in Mandy's life that she started having problems. She would become very anxious, and upset and would wet herself. After Mum had changed her, she would mess herself as well. This situation had been going on for a few months when Mum decided to take Mandy to see our family doctor about it as she was very concerned, it was most unusual. The doctor was very understanding about Mandy's problem, he suggested to Mum that she should go to see a specialist about it who may be able to help.

A few weeks later, Mum took me with her and Mandy to the hospital to see this doctor, he examined Mandy's tummy and other bodily parts. He did look rather puzzled about it, he told Mum that he felt that Mandy was very insecure, a very nervous, anxious little girl and when she felt this way, then she would have a little problem. He suggested that Mandy should be admitted to a specialist clinic for about 3-4 weeks, to be observed to see if her condition worsened or not. He told Mum that she could visit her any time of the day as there were no restrictions on visiting times there. After she had spent 3-4 weeks at this clinic, he would like to check her over to see how she was now feeling, after having therapy there on a daily basis.

Me and Mum visited Mandy, Mum would always take her some bubble bath, as Mandy did love to have a bath and being talked to afterwards. The specialist told Mum that Mandy was very insecure because of the situation with her dad and everything that had happened following her birth; somehow she had picked up on this. I suppose that both her brothers leaving like they did would not have helped either. Sometimes babies are aware of things like this, perhaps Mum too was feeling insecure, having to bring up another man's child on her own again. We had no father figure as a role model to look up to, so Mum became both, being a carer, a provider, a mother and a father all in one. Looking back, it must have been a very difficult job for her on her own, with no one to fall back on for support. The main thing was that she loved us all very much, she was always there for us and she did the very best for all her children. We did not have much in the way of money or possessions but what we did have was of so much more value.

So me and Mum would go on an evening about 4 times a week to visit Mandy. I really enjoyed travelling on the bus. Tony would stay with our next-door neighbour and catch up on his homework, perhaps watch some of the football on television, as he was mad keen on football, especially Man United whom he supported. After the four weeks ended, Mandy was assessed at the clinic to check and see if the therapy had helped her with her personal problem. Our next-door neighbour came to see Mum the very next day to say that there was a phone call, it was from the clinic. Mum was informed that Mandy was well enough now to come home and that could Mum call to take her home, either that day or the following day.

When Mum returned, she was very pleased with this news, she told me and Tony that we would be getting our little sister back that day. So, a few hours later, after she had cooked our tea, she set off with me in tow whilst Tony stayed back, probably watching television. After a nice bus ride to the clinic, Mum took Mandy's pram onto the ward to find Mandy settled and giggling with one of the nurses there, it was good to see her happy, even more so when she saw Mum. Around 15 minutes later, we were all on the bus back home. Mum was concerned that Mandy needed a feed, so as we got inside, the first thing that she did was feed and change Mandy, as she did this, Mum sang a nice happy little song. Tony came running in, straight over to look at Mandy, he gave her a squeeze, trying to tickle her, which she liked. I guess like me he was pleased to have her home again. To this very day, Mandy never knew about her time spent at this clinic, being too young, she would not remember it.

Autumn came and went, leaving winter just around the corner. Once again it was quite a cold winter, we had a lot of snow that year, ice too with biting northerly winds which did not help. My school was badly affected by the snow, so much so that it had to close, as did Tony's school. Snow disrupted the buses, even the electricity cables, so Mum went to the local shops to stock up on candles for us in case the power had to be cut off. We would be left with no power in the home, at least we had a gas oven, which meant that Mum could cook on that and boil water on the rings, so we could all have a cup of tea or a hot drink. This really bad weather lasted well over Christmas time, right into the new year in fact. Me and Tony did not mind though as we got to stay off school. However, after a few weeks, we both got rather bored and fed up.

There was no football played due to the pitch being full of snow and ice, so Tony was not pleased about this, though he did keep himself occupied by playing marbles on our lounge carpet. I went to my bedroom to play with my dolls, toys and teddies. I much preferred to be on my own with my own company as sometimes Tony and Mandy could be too much for me. Mum would sit by our gas fire at night, doing her knitting; she sometimes watched the news at the same time. Then, after getting all of us settled down for bed, she would either listen to the radio or read one of her many library books. Mum loved to read, especially adventure, true life stories, or family stories. In those days, families did things together, they made their own amusement and it did not always centre around watching television.

It was now approaching Mum's birthday in March. Her friend came round one day with a card and present for her, they sometimes had a small sherry or Babycham, just to toast a birthday, though Mum did not drink anyway, she never liked alcohol. It is a good job she didn't as our dad drank enough for the both of them. Mum received a card from our Darren which was nice, at least she was in his thoughts. Nothing from Simon though. One of Mum's male friends came round too, it was her dancing partner, he brought some chocolates for her, which she liked. Mum did miss her dancing, she was a very good dancer, though really it was more of a sociable evening out for her.

However, after Mum's birthday, around 3 weeks later, she went out to go dancing. Her friend said that she would look after Mandy, Tony and me for just a few hours. Mandy cried and cried all the time that Mum was away from home, this really concerned Mum's friend as each time she went to check on Mandy, the crying would stop and she would be giggling away. When Mum returned home that evening, her friend told her about it. She said that Mandy just cried all the time for some attention and when it was given, she was fine.

A few weeks later, Mum decided to go to an evening class with her friend, as she wanted to learn dress-making. Our neighbour from next door said she would look in on me and Mandy. But before Mum had even got out of the front door, Mandy started screaming, crying her eyes out, this really affected me, as like Mandy I felt insecure and clingy to Mum. Looking back, it is no wonder that me and Mandy were very insecure in ourselves, having one parent as our main care-giver this was quite understandable. The other thing was that up to this point, Mum had never really had a social life, all she did was cook, clean, feed and care for all 4 of us now on her own with no adult support, only her friends that helped her out. Thinking about the situation, I feel that all 5 of us were affected in some way, mainly due to the absence of a father, though on saying this, Mum really did a great job of bringing all of us up and keeping us together as a family. When Mandy played her up, it really upset me to see her like that, this played on my mind. When Mum returned that night, she looked in on us both. Well, Mandy was all smiles, giggling away in her bed as if nothing had happened.

Winter was with us once again; the weather then changed and we had rain, wind, then hailstones, and snow was on the way after the hailstones. That year it did snow in December, also around Christmas time. Mum would always make us pillowcases to put all our presents in, she would put all our names on them, ready to hang them up over the fireplace. We were always excited when Christmas came; sometimes me and Tony would try to stay awake to wait to see Santa Claus come down the chimney and take a sip of the sherry drink which Mum had left out for him, along with a handmade mince pie, which he always seemed to eat.

Mum was a great cook, always making her own Christmas cake, mince pies and jam tarts, she would even make Christmas cakes for a few of our neighbours, also her friends. Grandma and Grandad would always call to see Mum around 2 weeks before Christmas, usually when me and Tony were at school. They would bring us a Christmas gift each, giving Mum some money for her to treat herself to something she needed, which she never did. She always spent the money on her family. It went into the housekeeping pot.

Dad never ever sent us any kind of gifts or cards, we never received anything at all from him. At that time, he was working as an electrician which he had trained for, he was a good electrician when he was sober. But due to his drink problem, he had lost so many jobs; whilst at work, he could not pass a pub without going into it.

That year we all had a good Christmas. We opened our sacks, Mum had put some oranges and tangerines in each one, a little gift for us, Grandma's gift too, so we all had something to open on the big day. After that, we would have breakfast, get dressed, and go to play with our toys, until it was time for lunch.

Mum would not cook much for lunch, we just had a sandwich or perhaps bread and jam; our Tony really did have a good appetite. After lunch, we would watch television while Mum would listen to the radio, singing away to the Christmas songs. Mandy would always have an afternoon nap on Mum's bed, then it would be time for dinner where we had our big Christmas meal, usually a chicken, with roasted potatoes, sprouts, carrots, peas, chicken gravy, Yorkshire puddings; the chicken would be tender and very tasty. After this, we would be given Christmas pudding, nice, hot, sweet and sticky, we would always check to see if there was a sixpence inside it. When we had all finished, Mum would bring out the lovely Christmas cake, cut a slice for each of us and a tiny piece for herself. So, as you can see, although poor Mum always made sure that we had enough food to eat, never going without, the only person who went without was Mum herself.

We always came home from school to a home-cooked meal each day, a nice warm home, plenty of attention, plenty of love to go around, these were the main things we needed. When Christmas was over, we were approaching the new year, another new year, though it was still very cold outside, Mum would go to the local shop which was around 10 minutes' walk away. I was not allowed to go out in the cold because I was prone to catching colds, which would often turn into a chest infection that I did not want.

6

Then before we knew it, both me and Tony were back at school after our Christmas break. I was around 7½ years old now, so I still had a few more years to go before I went to the big school. Tony was already there, he really liked school, he was quite bright, a quiet thoughtful boy and well-liked, he always had plenty of friends, unlike me. I was a very shy, introverted, sulky girl who did not make friends easily. I was never very sociable, preferring my own company. I guess that I was complex, I never liked too many people around me, I could not really relate to people and I was quite a miserable, sad person. As the years went by, I became more unsociable, especially during my teenage years.

Mandy was about 4 years old at that time, once again, like my brothers, I did not have much time for her. I somehow knew from an early age that we were not genuine sisters, though we did look alike; when Mum used to dress us in the same outfits, people used to think that we were twins, as Mandy was a big-built, tall girl for her age and I was the opposite, a tiny, slight, petite, skinny girl.

Springtime was here, I liked the spring, we would all be dressed smart and go to the park which we all enjoyed. Sometimes Tony would not come with us, as he wanted to go play with his mates, usually returning home when he was hungry. Mum had a very big garden to look after, which she loved doing. She would spend the best part of a day in it, digging, weeding, planting and even growing her own vegetables, they were delicious. It must have been very difficult for her as she had no help to cut the lawn or any of the other jobs she did out there. I never ever saw any of my brothers helping her to do the garden. I know Mandy and I never did.

She painted and decorated the whole house herself, this again she really enjoyed doing and seeing the fruits of her labour afterwards. Mum was a very independent woman so looking back, perhaps she never asked any of my brothers for help with the garden. I do know she never asked me or Mandy though I feel that we should have offered. I too enjoy my independence. In the past, I have been too proud to ask for help, perhaps that's where I get it from.

When they lived at home, my brothers had white pet rabbits in hutches outside which sometimes Mum ended up having to clean out, when they forgot to do it. They also had a lot of white mice which in time had multiplied, like they do, so Mum asked them if they could give some to their friends, or perhaps the school, as we did not have the space to keep anymore. Both me and Mandy were too young at the time to have pets, though I always loved animals from being little, I liked the cute, cuddly, soft ones. Tony liked animals too, he did rescue a little bird which had a broken wing. At the time he made a small box for it, fed it regularly, and cared for and looked after it for weeks until its wing became mended, then he released it back into the garden area. After that it would come back and land on our kitchen windowsill, looking for him, it would not forget all his tender care.

That year the summer was quite hot with long, sunny days, blue skies and plenty of those pesky little midges and flies which really bothered us, especially when they landed in our hair, we had to brush our hair like mad to get rid of them. By this time, Mum had met a very nice gentleman friend who would take us all out in his car to the nearest seaside, where we would all walk along the promenade, he would buy us all an ice cream and we would sit down to enjoy the view. Mum really enjoyed those days out, as we did, the car ride was great too, as we got to see some of the countryside, which I liked and still do to this day. Although we lived on an estate in a town, I much prefer the countryside with all the varied birds and animals, plenty going on every day, also every season. I am not a townie kind of person, as I love nature, and animals too much. I am really at home in the country.

The summer of 1969 was a very long, hot one. We had a few trips to the seaside, Mum would make us all some sandwiches, homemade buns and crisps. She would include orange juice and a cake which was nice. If we were still hungry after all this, then Mum's gentleman friend would treat us all to fish and chips, sometimes shrimps which I did not really like, too fiddly to eat, although with the fish, I always had to debone it, as I hated all the little bones. This has always stuck with me right up to today.

Before we knew it, autumn was fast approaching. Mum would be out in the garden, tidying up and cutting the grass amongst all her other jobs, she really was a hard worker. She would make sure that although I would walk to school which was around 3 – 4 miles round trip every day, she would always collect me and walk back home with me, carrying my satchel for me, pushing Mandy in her pram at the same time. However, this one year I remember well that at my school we had a playground with swings in it. I loved to go on a swing, well this particular day, I swung too high in the air. I became very unbalanced and fell off the swing landing on the pavement, in doing so I broke my arm. My teacher rang our next-door neighbour to inform Mum of my accident. She ran all the way to my school, where an ambulance had been sent for. We both went inside, I did not realise at that time that I had broken my arm, as I did not feel anything when it happened.

At the hospital, I was taken for an x-ray which confirmed the break. I was put in plaster of Paris for about 8 weeks or so until the broken bone had mended. The nurse told me that I was very brave as she handed me a lollipop. The break was in my right arm and as I am right-handed, I was unable to use it, so Mum decided that I should take time off school until it had thoroughly mended. I did not mind this, though due to my ongoing health problems over the years, I had missed a lot of my schooling, so I had to try and catch up which was quite hard for me to do.

During the 8 weeks, I became very bored being at home, I could not even go out to play. This is what I missed more than anything else. The day finally came when it was time for me to have my cast removed. Boy was I glad when it was taken off my arm. Oh! It felt so good. So, now I could go back to school and play outside, it was so great to get back to doing something again.

It just meant that I had a lot of catching up to do on my schoolwork which I really tried to do every day.

October was just around the corner, which meant that my 8th birthday was near. I really loved birthdays, I wondered what it would bring. My brother Simon came with presents that year, though once again he and Mum had heated words in the kitchen and he did not stay long. I believe my presents were from my grandparents, not him as he was still living with them at that time. I had quite a few birthday cards that year and as I opened one of them, I noticed on the envelope it was addressed to my mum, not me, so I went and gave it to her. Upon reading the letter, she became very excited and told us that she had won a holiday abroad in a competition she had taken part in earlier in the year.

Well, you could imagine how Mum felt, she had never in her life won anything, let alone a holiday. She asked Tony to look after me and Mandy as she had a phone call to make. She ran all the way up to the top of our road, to a pay phone to ring the phone number in the letter, which was to confirm that she really had won this, all expenses paid holiday for two adults. The man on the phone said that it was genuine, and told her that the holiday had to be taken from January the following year until October that same year. It was for 2 adults, so did Mum have anyone in mind, a friend perhaps who she could take with her? She said that she would have a think about it and get back to them in a few days.

She decided to ring a very good male friend whom she had met at a dance to ask if he would like to go abroad with her. Judging by the quick time it took her to return home from the payphone, I guess that the answer was no. Mum was in a quandary as to what to do. Oh! There really was so much for her to think about, the main question being just who could she take? After a few days, she decided to meet her very good female friend whom she had known since my birth. She had been quite poorly lately, so Mum was still unsure whether to ask her or not. She came back from her phone call looking very pleased with herself, and told me, Mandy and Tony that next year, she and her friend would be going away on a holiday abroad, well who would have thought it? The furthest Mum had travelled to at that time was our local seaside around 30 miles away, she was just so excited about it.

The next few days Mum spent telling all her dancing friends and our neighbours about her winning a holiday abroad. Mum's friend, Brenda, decided to visit her that day to go over everything, to look at the holiday brochure for them to make a decision as to where they would like to go. They did this over a cup of tea, they sat in our large kitchen with an equally large handmade wooden table with all the brochures spread out and open. Brenda was quite excited about it too, although she had travelled abroad before so she was no stranger to different cultures and traditions. Anyway, about 2 hours or so later, they both had come to a decision that they would be going to Spain for 3 weeks at the end of January 1970. This would be a holiday to remember for Mum as she really did need a breakaway, it would do her the world of good also the lovely Spanish sunshine too.

Then after that, Mum said that she needed to earn some spending money for the trip, so what could she do to earn some much-needed pennies? As she was a wonderful hand knitter, there was an opportunity which came up in our local wool shop; they needed someone to knit baby clothes, bonnets, mittens, bootees etc. The pay was not much, it just depended on how many one could knit in a week. When the representative next visited the wool shop, Mum went to see him with the baby clothes she had knitted. The rep was very pleased with all the garments. Throughout October, November and December, all Mum seemed to be doing was knitting, knitting, knitting, most days also nights.

January arrived at last, it was only 16 days to go until Mum flew, for the very first time, to Spain with her friend, Brenda. She was a little bit apprehensive about the flight, though Brenda reassured her everything would be alright. Me and Mandy were to stay with one of Mum's other friends, who had 2 children of her own. Tony was to stay with a neighbour from the old estate we used to live on. So that was everything settled, Viva Espana here we come. Both Mum and Brenda were flying from Heathrow airport, so they were given a lift there by Brenda's husband. Mum came and gave us all a cuddle, said all her goodbyes with tears in her eyes and told us to be good for her friends and then they were on their way.

7

Viva Espana

The 3 weeks that Mum was away really dragged by for us. By the end of it, both me and Mandy were fed up with the same meals being served to us every day by Mum's friend, who was no cook like Mum who could turn her hand to anything. I guess that at home we were just spoilt for choice. Mum's friend drove us home and when we arrived we found Mum looking very brown, sun-kissed, calm, relaxed and very happy, she looked so well and was pleased to see us all. Looking back, I guess that the holiday was just what the doctor ordered. Tony came running up to her and asked,

"What's for tea mum?"

Like me and Mandy, he too missed her cooking.

That year was quite a warm, settled one. Easter time was always pleasant, we would go to our local park, sometimes having a day out at the seaside, when Mum's gentleman friend was not working. We all enjoyed the seaside, the sunshine and the beach, though not the sand between my toes, which I hated and spent a lot of my time trying to get rid of it. Mum would always buy us an ice cream, sometimes going without herself, as she just did not have the money. She would buy 2 bags of chips for us to share amongst ourselves. She had a budget for our little seaside trips, though we always had a good time. It was nice for her to have a break from working, cooking, cleaning and caring for us. If it had not been for her gentleman friend, we would never have been able to go away on these day trips as even a weekend away at the seaside was just beyond Mum's means.

The summer was over too soon that year, we reminisced about the lovely day trips to the seaside, the sand castles, the ice creams, the donkeys, seagulls and of course paddling in the sea. Oh! It was just so good to get away!

By this time, Mandy was around 5 years old, ready to start school in September, she was a very big, well-built girl, looking older for her age, unlike me. However, like Tony, she too had developed a big appetite. I will say this for all my siblings, they all enjoyed their food. I, on the other hand, was still very picky with my food, though not as bad as when I was very young.

My two older brothers both had girlfriends by now, they never visited as much, only on birthdays and Christmas time, though not every year. Tony was now around 13 years old, a teenager, he was a very popular boy at school, quiet and calm, he did have a lot of friends and he would sometimes bring them back home for a feast when Mum was making toffee apples for us, there they would be all lined up, ready to dive in and enjoy.

September arrived, it was mild at the start, like me I guess that Mandy would be nervous too, having to leave the safety of our home, the security of Mum always being there for us. I wondered how she would cope, as I did not fare too well on my first day. The good thing about it was that my school was next door to Mandy's so I could collect her before Mum came to take us home. In time, as we grew older, Mum would rely on me to collect Mandy and walk her home. She soon got used to school, as I did at this time. However, I did find some of the subjects there very difficult for me, so I was allowed a longer time to complete my learning. I was quite slow at picking things up and understanding a new subject. I was not allowed to participate in any form of physical education so I just had to sit out and watch all my classmates enjoying themselves. In a way, this made me feel like the odd one out, as it were, and intriguing to some of them. I was often questioned as to why I was not allowed to join in.

I did have a few favourite subjects, whilst at school, one being English. I liked history and music too although I disliked science, I could not understand it at all. Maths was okay, though what I really did enjoy was English, in particular, writing essays and short stories.

Winter was now back, it brought with it the cold north wind, we also had some snow that year. Before we knew it, Christmas was upon us again. Simon came to visit us that year, with presents for all of us. He now had a good job and was aiming to buy his own home in time, he did not want to live in a council house like us, he somehow thought it was beneath him and he told my mum this on many occasions. Mum and Simon were in the kitchen having words once again, this occurred most times when they met, though at that time I was too young to understand what it was all about. However Darren, Tony, me and Mandy were all very afraid of him, as he had such a forceful nature, almost bitter, he had a lot of anger in him, most of it was directed at Mum.

Mum too had a similar nature; she became the only one of us who could talk back to him. She was not frightened of him, unlike us, she was not afraid of anyone, let alone her oldest son. Looking back, I expect that this had to do with the survival spirit she gained whilst in care as a young girl, she learned to stick up for herself, to fight for what she wanted and she would never ever let anyone put her down.

We had a nice, pleasant Christmas that year, despite Simon and Mum's little tête-a-tête, he only came for a few hours, it was just as well, as we were all pleased when he had gone. By now the year was 1971. I would be 10 years old in October, it was the year that I remember when I came to like music. Mum had a radio that one of her many friends had bought her, she would often sing to the songs around our home, whilst doing her chores so it was often on and I came to enjoy listening to it as well.

Eastertime that year was good as we always had a visit from Grandma and Grandad, armed with plenty of easter eggs for us. Mum would make them afternoon tea, with cakes, and various sandwiches, lots of biscuits, jam tarts, for us all to tuck into and enjoy. We always received an Easter egg, well me and Mandy anyway, Tony being older going on 14 years old, was given a choice of either a visit to the pictures or a large bar of chocolate. He usually plumped for the pictures which in those days were rather good and very popular with families. He would go with a few of his friends from school, sometimes coming home with some popcorn that he had saved for us.

Mandy's birthday was nice, being in June, the weather was fairly warm. Mum made her a little birthday cake with some candles, she would always help her blow them out. Growing up, Mandy was a happy, pleasant girl who for some reason I never knew why, I resented. I guess that I felt jealous of her, though I do think that at an early age, she picked up on this, as we never ever saw eye to eye with each other. We were like chalk and cheese, never close, looking back I do feel that this was my fault, as in those days, I was very prickly, sensitive, defensive, and an angry child with a very unpleasant nature. I was not nice to know at all, growing up. As I became older, I developed a nasty, selfish, self-absorbed personality, bitter if you like, a little like my older brother Simon, though on saying this, I have never, ever in my 59 years met anyone quite like Simon, he was a one-off. Like Simon, I did not have many friends, I was a loner, liking my own company. Me and Mandy would argue constantly, mainly this was to do with our bedroom which we shared. My side was always tidy whereas hers was scruffy, most times I would end up cleaning it. We did not like the same things, interests etc, but unlike me, Mandy was clever and intelligent, she would easily learn new things.

That year I remember Mum bought me a beautiful pram for my lovely doll to go in, this was a special present for my 10th birthday. I would go around the living room pushing it about, much to Mandy and Simon's annoyance, as he had come to give me a present for my birthday. I suddenly had an accident with the pram, I accidentally pushed it into Mum's new sideboard. Well, Simon went mad, shouting at me and Mum, saying that I was very clumsy and did not appreciate such a lovely toy. Once again, he spoilt my birthday with his outburst, like he often did. Well both me and Mum were upset, this really did cause an awful atmosphere within our family unit. After his outbursts, he never stayed long. He did not visit us at Christmas that year, in a way I do feel that most of us were glad about this.

The New Year of 1972 arrived and with it, a dusting of snow, which Mum tried to clear so that we children would be able to walk down our long path. The snow I did not mind, it was the ice

I did not like, it could be dangerous, especially on the roads, if you were driving.

Me and Mandy were on our way to school one day, we were walking on the snow which had laid thick about 6 inches deep at that time and we were messing around, making snowballs like children do. We both enjoyed playing with the snow and throwing the snowballs at each other. Anyway, to avoid one, I jumped on what I thought was the edge of the path. As I did so, I hit a big icy patch, which someone had been trying to skate on, so as you can imagine, it was very slippery and dangerous. The next thing I knew, I had gone up, fallen on top of the ice, cut my chin open and there was blood, blood everywhere. As we were so near to our school, Mandy ran to the school to get some help for me. Mum was sent for, as was an ambulance, which took us both to the A and E Department at the nearest hospital. Everyone was rushing about and then I was taken into a side room. A nice doctor came in and explained to me and Mum exactly what had happened to me and she said that I would need some stitches in my chin. I was to be a brave little girl, to which I nodded a yes, well I was brave, afterwards I was given a little lollipop as my reward.

Me, Mandy and Mum returned home after spending 3 hours at the hospital. I had a dressing on my chin which did hurt, though it did not stop me from eating my tea that night. I was kept off school for a few days after my accident and ever since that time, I have been very scared of the ice. I still have the scar on my chin from that accident. Anyway, when Simon found out about my accident, he was annoyed at Mum for not letting him know earlier as he now had a car, he said that he would have taken us to the hospital. Mum told him that if any of us ever had another accident in or outside the home, she would contact him straight away. So, after that, I always avoided any ice on the path or road, wherever there was ice, I avoided it, come what may.

The snow and ice came and went that year, the spring was lovely once again. By that time, Tony had become very interested in girls, as 14-year-old boys do. Simon had visited us the week before we had our half-term school holiday to tell us the good news that he was now engaged to a lovely young lady and that they were to be married the following year, in the summer. He asked Mum if both me and Mandy could be their bridesmaids and she agreed of course. Well, when we were told of this, we were both very excited indeed as we had never been bridesmaids before. The material was to be provided for us and we would be required to go for a few fittings before they were made. Mum was quite excited too. Having met Simon's intended a few weeks before the announcement, Mum thought that Linda was too high class for Simon, completely in a different league to him, she was quite posh too.

They did not exactly get off to a good start, as Simon had stated that as Mum lived in a council house, we did not have many possessions, no carpets, he was quite ashamed of us, it was him that was the snob, not Linda, as she did accept us as we were.

The summer was lovely and hot that year, 1972, Mandy had a nice, relaxing birthday with toys she enjoyed playing with, especially her little piano which Mum had saved up to pay for, that was her favourite gift. Mum always did her best for us, buying lovely gifts.

8

School's Out

The summer holidays felt extremely long; we were off school for 8 weeks, way, way too long I thought and I was really glad to return to school that year, as me, Mandy and Tony were all doing well. We were always so smart and tidy in ourselves, due to Mum knitting all our jumpers and making sure that our shoes were shiny and clean; she really was very proud of how we were turned out.

My 11th birthday was good, though we had no visit from Simon or Darren, who did not call to see us all much anyway, just on the odd occasion such as our birthdays or Christmas. Mum really missed both my older brothers though she never spoke much about them to us. Darren now had a nice girlfriend, unfortunately, like my Dad, he had developed a taste for alcohol. Also, like Dad, he wanted to join the Navy which he did eventually. This meant that he was away from home a lot and when he did pay us a visit, Mum did not recognise him as he was no longer the thoughtful, loving, caring young boy who ran away to a better life with his dad, or so he thought. Sadly, he had become like a complete clone of our dad. She was very disappointed in him indeed as out of us all, Darren had always been her favourite.

Before we all knew it, winter was upon us once again, with the usual snowfall which living in the north of England we got used to. It covered the ground and lay around 6 inches deep, so the main path which led to our house at the end was like an ice skating rink, due to all our neighbours' children running up and down it. I now walked on the side of the path, I was not taking any chances that year, as I did not want a repeat of my fall from the previous year.

Christmas was a quiet time for us all that year. Simon did visit us, he brought his fiancé to meet us, she seemed quite nice, too good for him, I thought. Once more they did not stay long. I could feel that Mum was not very comfortable with him being there, perhaps because of his nasty, cold previous comment about our council house. This is how he made all of us feel most of the time as he would say things without thinking about them first, this could be hurtful and offensive, not only that, according to Simon, whatever he said was always right; one of the reasons he and Mum would argue, he just could not bear to be told.

As the wedding was to be in June of 1972, both me and Mandy were looking forward to having our dressing fittings. Mum of course would be buying a new outfit and making a dress herself for the evening of the wedding.

January came and went, spring was here at last. Mum had planted lots of different bulbs in the rockery area of our large back garden. She had planted a variety of vegetables too, such as potatoes, carrots, peas, cauliflower and lettuce though not much fruit, although we did have a nice gooseberry bush in the corner of the garden which Mum would make us gooseberry crumble with, it was so delicious with custard.

We all would go to the park at Easter time, though this year as a treat for us all, Darren said that he would pay for us to go to the local pictures. We saw 2 lovely family films, which we children really enjoyed, as Mum did too, and it made a change for her to be able to dress up and go out somewhere.

Now May was on the horizon, as was mine and Mandy's dress fittings for the wedding. The colour was so lovely, a light jade colour, it had white flowers around the neck and waist, the length was full right to the ground. Mandy would always begin to fidget, moving around, she was not keen on dresses, preferring skirts and tops like me. Mum had been clothes shopping a week before we had our fittings. She had settled on a sweet white 2 piece suit, skirt, top and a little bolero jacket to go with it. She told us that she hoped it would be suitable for the occasion as she did not want to outdo the bride.

Simon's fiancé, Linda, had decided that she would have 3 bridesmaids, one being her best friend from school, Suzy, who was a nice, kind, intelligent girl and of course me and Mandy. Simon had decided that his best friend, Pete, would be his best man, not one of his brothers. However, Darren did not want to go to the wedding as he was away at sea at that time.

The wedding day arrived and we were all very nervous, especially Mum. We all had our hair done at our local hair salon. Me and Mandy had long hair at the time, so the stylist took it high up and held it on top with little hair clips with white flowers on them; she pinned them all along our hair. Mum also had little white flowers pinned in her hair too. She really did look beautiful that day and very proud too. Our dad, it seemed, was not invited, which for us was good as he could not be trusted to be around alcohol anyway.

The wedding car arrived early for me and Mandy. We were very excited by it all, Mum and Tony were given a lift by one of Mum's friends. Well, we arrived at the church around 20 minutes later, the church was quite small, though I could see that Linda had just arrived with her father. She looked so happy and radiant. Both me and Mandy were instructed to walk behind the bride down the long aisle, where at the end Simon and his best man had been waiting around 10 minutes. He looked very nervous, though the sight of his bride-to-be soon calmed him down.

The whole process took around 45 minutes, the married couple having signed the register, they both made their way back down the aisle, so this was Mandy's and my cue to join them along with Suzy, the maid of honour. Mandy started fidgeting once again, pulling her dress, so Suzy turned round and told her to stop doing it. Then as we all got outside the church, there were 2 local photographers there, clicking away with their big cameras. They wanted me and Mandy to stand together for a shot, which we did and then it was my turn to disappear, which I did, I could not get away from them quick enough. Suzy had around 4 photos taken and Mandy around 6 or 7 photos as she did not mind having her photo taken. I just had a couple of photos taken as I did not like being photographed, this has stayed with me right up to today.

However, the complete family photograph was rather interesting, as I was the only one of the family not on it. Simon once again had something to say to me after the photographs were developed, though I did expect that he would anyway. The reception was very good, there were a lot of guests, the food was pretty good too, as was the wedding cake. Me and Mandy were allowed to have a tiny taste of the Champagne, Mum had some too, though as she did not drink, she preferred to have a small sherry, which was more to her liking.

The evening came, there was some good music played and a disco, which we all enjoyed as did Mum, in fact, she had quite a lot of dances. Her handmade evening dress was lovely, it was made of velour, with an abstract pattern on it and Linda's mum commented on how nice it was. Mum's friend came to collect me, Tony and Mandy, around 8 pm to take us home. It had been a very, very long day for all of us. Mum said that she would only stay for a few more hours and come to look in on us when she returned.

As Tony was 15 years old, he was allowed to stay up until 9 p.m. We were so tired out when we got home, just time for a nightcap, some hot chocolate in our case, a wash, brush our teeth and into bed, we both went. By the time Mum looked in on us, around 10.15 p.m., we were both spark out, so she was not too late to bed either that night. As it was the weekend, we could all have a lie-in, at least until around 9 a.m. Mum was up and about by the time we got dressed, Tony was sitting at the kitchen table, we could smell something nice to eat, fried bread and boiled eggs, not forgetting the little soldiers which we liked. Mum was unusually quiet, perhaps it was because of the after-effects of the wedding, as it had been a very long, tiring though pleasant day for all of us. Nothing was said about the wedding in the weeks that followed. Soon both me, Mandy and Tony would return to school, after being off for 8 weeks, school holidays.

Tony was now 16 years old, so he had a decision to make if he wanted to stay on at school or go to college to further his education. He chose to leave school and train to be a mechanic and went to night college to learn a trade. He attended a technical college, 3 evenings a week for 6 to 8 months. Mum would always be there when he returned home around 8.30 p.m. to cook him some dinner and then he would settle down in front of the television to watch some football, while we entertained ourselves with other things. Tony sometimes stayed up until late at night to watch a film, usually a French-subtitled one which he liked. After 3 months of leaving school, he managed to find a full-time job, though he still went to night college. Mum was pleased that he had a job now, also he started seeing a new girlfriend, whom he would see every Friday night.

Mum always went out dancing on a Friday night, so Tony would look after us 2 girls; we had to be in bed no later than 9 p.m. Mandy did not like this idea but I was not really bothered, then he would bring his girlfriend back and they would watch television together. Her name was Vickey. Mum had been able to meet her the week before. I do not think that she approved of her though, it was hard for Mum to adapt to all these new people in her life. Also when we were introduced to her, Mandy just pulled a face. I thought she was too loud and brash for Tony, as he had always been a quiet, easy-going, shy, thoughtful boy.

My birthday came around again. Mum as usual bought me some lovely useful gifts, as did Tony.

9 - Family ties

Towards the end of October, it was a Saturday and there was a knock at the front door. Mum always answered it, she was usually in the kitchen baking a cake or something for our tea and did not really like being interrupted. Me and Mandy were outside playing at the time. Tony was up in his bedroom and Mum shouted up to him that he had a visitor, so he ran downstairs to come face to face with Dad, who was standing in the kitchen, so Mum shut the door to allow them to talk privately. Up to this point in our lives, Dad had never before come to see Tony or made any contact with me. It seemed now that Tony had turned 16 years old and was working, he wanted to get to know him, to have him in his life. Anyway, Mum heard raised voices coming from the kitchen. Tony was not happy, he stormed out of the kitchen and gave Mum a quick glance before heading to the stairs to his bedroom.

Mum saw Dad out and went up to have a word with Tony who was very upset about the situation. They had a long talk and he told Mum that Dad was interested in him and wanted to get to know him more, to which Tony had replied, "You have had 16 years to get to know me, why now?" Tony told his dad that he was not interested in getting to know him; anyway, he smelt of alcohol so no change there then.

The winter came, it was a mild one, with hardly any snow and ice which I was glad about. Christmas was just a few weeks away when Tony asked Mum if it was alright if Vickey, his girlfriend, could come over on Boxing Day, both Simon and Linda would be visiting too, along with Mum's new boyfriend, also his 2 children. So, we would be having quite a houseful. Mum said that she did not mind in the least, as she would say to us, "the more the merrier". There were 10 people for Mum to cook for. Tony gave her a little more housekeeping money, which would help. Mum would always bake a Christmas cake for us, of course, and the next-door neighbour, some of her friends and her boyfriend and his family.

We spent Christmas Day together, just the 4 of us, which was nice, then we watched a few Christmas films together, the Queen's speech and a carol-singing service. We all anticipated what Boxing Day would bring, especially as Simon would be coming. He arrived first with some gifts, then Mum's boyfriend with his 2 children. The last ones to arrive were Tony and his girlfriend, Vickey, they travelled on the bus, unlike Simon and Linda who came in a car. After all the introductions, we settled down to the lovely meal that Mum had made for us. Her boyfriend's children were the first to finish. Simon surprised us with some good news, Linda was expecting. This really did please Mum as it would be her first grandchild. Linda was unable to have a drink as Mum reached for the sherry that she always kept in the house, especially for Christmas time.

Vickey was knocking back the sherry, perhaps to give her some Dutch courage after meeting Simon. Most people upon meeting Simon for the first time were quite nervous and tense, he certainly was not the easiest person to get on with. I thought he was very complex with various issues. Mum's boyfriend on the other hand was a very nice, shy kind of man, so he did not have much to say to any of our family. However, Simon did have a quiet word with Mum concerning his 2 children who had finished off all the sandwiches and were now wolfing down the Christmas cake, before moving on to the cheese and biscuits. Good job Mum made a lot of each.

Around 8.30 p.m., Mum's boyfriend decided to call it a night and head home. His youngest at that time was only 5 years old, so he needed to get him to bed. Then a little later on, Simon said that they should be getting back too, and asked Tony if Vickey would like a lift home, or if were they planning on catching the bus. Tony decided that it would be best if Vickey had a lift home, as it was rather cold and dark outside so they all left together. Mum set to, washing all the pots and pans and tidying up. She did not mind as she really enjoyed entertaining. Tony thanked Mum for making Vickey feel very welcome and also for all the food that she had made for us, then off he went into the living room to watch some television. As it was now past 9 o'clock, me and

Mandy made our way to bed. We were rather tired but Mandy was excited about the new baby, talking about Vickey who she liked, and said that she was good for Tony too. Mum never said much about the meal or Simon's comments concerning her boyfriend's children who I thought were very well-behaved, like most children with a good appetite.

Christmas flew by that year before we were aware of it and the New Year had come and gone too. It was time for me and Mandy to go back to school, after the holidays. We both wore our new hats, gloves and scarves, which Mum had knitted for us.

Spring was now on the way, my favourite time of the year, not so much the Easter time though. I did enjoy all the Easter eggs, as did Mandy. The weather was quite mild too, which was so nice, it meant that we could all go to the big park in the town, which had a lot more swings and rides. Mum always made sure that we were safe on them, as Tony was 16 years old, he no longer came to the park with us, he much preferred the company of his friends from school or college, though most of his time was spent with his girlfriend, Vickey. Mum seemed to sense some jealousy from her, as Tony and Mum looked so much alike, a lot more than any of us really. He was a handsome young man, with lovely dark curly hair and big blue eyes; he had a nice, kind face I thought.

His girlfriend Vickey was rather plain, on the plump side, with straight blond hair. Mandy was in awe of her, as she was so very confident in herself and came over a lot older than Tony, though she was only 6 months older than him. I got the impression that Vickey could be flirty with other young men. I do know she liked a good drink, perhaps this was the reason Mum never really took to her.

One of Mum's friends had a small caravan at the seaside and she told Mum that we could use it to go on holiday in the summer this year. Mum told us this after we had finished our tea that night. Well, as you can imagine, we were very excited about going away on holiday having never spent a week away at the seaside before. We would be travelling there by train, so Mum started saving there and then for our train fare, though she told her friend that we could only stay for a long weekend due to the financial situation. Well, this was all okay as me and Mandy would try to save up our pocket money to spend whilst there.

Half term came around once again for us and by this time, we had acquired a new friend in the form of a cute little puppy dog, which followed us everywhere. He even waited at the school gates for us. He lived at the end of the road and was just left on his own most days, his owners did not bother with him at all, so I guess he was lonely. He adopted me and Mandy. We were not allowed to let him in the house, but he really did enjoy our attention and company. We looked forward to seeing him every day. One day we were playing with Marley in the front garden when Simon dropped by for a visit. Well, he went mad to see us both playing with him and he shouted for Mum to come and look; he told both of us off, he really did make quite a scene, so much so that it got our neighbours' nets twitching. Anyway, after he left, Mum came to tell us that it was not a good idea for us to play with the dog as we did not know where he had been. His owners did not seem to care as to where he went, he was just left to take care of himself, roaming the streets most days. We both wanted a pet of our own, though we knew that Mum could not afford it, as we were going away for a weekend at the seaside. We both understood perhaps when we were a little older, we would be able to have a pet.

I had a little money box I would put my 50-pence pocket money into it each week, whereas Mandy would spend hers on lots of sweets so she never had any spending money.

May came and went and Mandy's 9th birthday was not far off. Perhaps Mum would buy her a little pet, I thought, as she was always on about wanting a hamster. Grandma and Grandad came the weekend before her birthday, they gave Mum some money, around £5 in today's money, this was really to help her out with the housekeeping, food and any other necessities, though she always did spend it on us. Mum decided to make us girls equal so a few days later, she suggested that we all got the bus into town to look at a new pet shop which had just opened. Well, we were both very excited about this.

It was a large shop with various fluffy, cute pets. There were guinea pigs, rabbits, mice, gerbils, hamsters and the like. There was an offer at the time, if you bought 2 it made it cheaper, so we ended up bringing home 2 hamsters, a cage, food and some bedding. Mum said that this was Mandy's birthday present also mine, though my birthday was not until October, so I did not mind having an early birthday present. We set the cage up in the indoor shed area. I decided to call my hamster "Hammy" and Mandy named hers "Sammy". They shared the same cage, though Hammy was a female and Sammy a male, they never had babies. Hammy and Sammy got on very well, we loved showing them off to the neighbours, though Mum and Tony were not too keen on them. The school holidays seemed to go too fast, though before we knew it, it was time to go away to the seaside.

10

July that year was a lovely sunny month off. We went on the train to the seaside, staying in a tiny, cramped caravan; though to us it did not matter as we loved the seaside. We really enjoyed the train journey there, not so much the caravan as it had no toilet, so we had to use the communal ones on the site, which was a bit of a nuisance, but something we got used to.

Whilst there, Mum became friendly with a man and his son who were staying in a caravan a few doors away from us. I did not really like the look of them. Also on the caravan site, there were nightly shows and entertainment which we went to. Mum met a man whilst there who bought her a drink, me and Mandy had a soft drink, while we all watched the entertainment.

Before we knew it, the time had come for us to go home, so we all packed our bags ready to leave. The man who had a son caught up with us on the way out of the caravan site and offered us a lift to the train station as our bags were heavy. Mum agreed, so off we all went. He made both me and Mum feel very uncomfortable. We were glad when we arrived at the station and Mum was quick to get out of his car, as she did so, she gave him a scowly look of annoyance. We said our goodbyes, then they went on their way back home. Mum gave a big sigh of relief, I think that she was pleased to see them leave. It turned out that he had propositioned Mum whilst at the site, not for himself but for his son. Mum was quite disgusted, annoyed and upset at this.

We were back on the train and home in no time at all. We had enjoyed a lovely break away but we were all looking forward to getting back to our own beds, and familiar daily routine. Tony had been looking after the house for us, also the 2 hamsters and he had invited Vickey round on a few occasions. She had made us a cake of some sort, which tasted horrible, so it went in the bin.

As me and Mandy shared a double bed at the time, I always liked to be neat and tidy. I went straight to my bedroom after being greeted by Tony. I checked our bedroom and found something there which did not belong to us, so I called Mum up to have a look. She had a displeased look on her face, though she never said anything to me. That night, I heard raised voices coming from the kitchen, it was Tony and Mum. Mandy wondered why there was all this shouting, of course, I knew, but did not tell her as she was too young at the time to hear such things. I was very annoyed with Tony for using our bedroom as he did, it was very disrespectful, as Mum put him on trust to look after the house, though young people will be young and do what they like I thought.

Then before we knew it, the lovely summer was drawing to a close and soon the new term would begin at school, also I would be a teenager in October, it would be my 13th birthday.

Tony now had a full-time job, though he still attended technical college in the evening. He was a brilliant artist, especially drawing with pencils. He made some wonderful sketches and drawings. I guess that both he and I inherited this from Mum as she was very artistic; having to be independent, she could paint, hang wallpaper, change a fuse and do manual jobs with ease, there was nothing really that she could not put her mind to. By this time, me and Mandy attended the same school. She went to the under 10 years junior school which was next door, so I would often see her in the playground.

It was mild for September that year. I had not been feeling too well for a few days, I had this stabbing pain in one of my knees, especially when bending down. I did this one evening whilst in the living room and the awful pain came on again. I felt faint, so I shouted to Mum who was very concerned and came running in.

"What's happened?" she said.

"I can't get up," I replied. "My knee joint somehow has locked."

Mum decided to go next door, as the neighbour had a phone. She returned to say that Simon was on his way and that we had to go to the hospital to have it checked out. Tony said that he would look after Mandy. Simon arrived and off we all went to the hospital. He carried me to the car. We arrived around 20 minutes later, to be seen by a doctor, who examined me, poked and prodded my knee, leg and ankle. He came to the conclusion that it was arthritis of some sort, they gave me some medication to take, advised Mum to keep an eye on me and then we left. Simon carried me to the car, he seemed rather annoyed at me for putting him out like this. Nothing was said on our way home. He carried me inside and placed me on the settee, whilst Mum went to get me a glass of water so that I could take my pills. This was the first time that I had heard of the complaint of arthritis, so did not know how to deal with it at that time. Simon and Mum had a little chat in the hall and then he was gone.

Mum said to me, "Perhaps it would be better to get you up to bed to get rested." So she helped me up the stairs and within 5 minutes I was safely settled in bed, glad to be home again.

The next day my knee felt a lot better and as it was the weekend, I did not have to go to school. Mandy went out to play, as usual. I decided to stay in and read one of my books. We belonged to the local library so that kept me busy for a few hours. As the weeks passed, my knee became less painful for me. As I enjoyed walking, I was as active as I could be, though at school I was not allowed to do any P.E., I just had to watch all my classmates from the sidelines.

One day, towards the end of September, Mum said to me that soon it would be my birthday. I knew that she could not afford much, though, like the others, she would always spoil me with a lovely tea, birthday cake and the like. From a very early age, I had a sweet tooth, so I did know what to expect from Mum. My birthday came round, the weather was very miserable, it usually was in October. Mum had heard from Darren who said that he would try to visit us. Grandma and Grandad came with gifts, also a gift for me from Simon, Tony and Mandy got me a card. Mum bought me a very useful gift which I liked, all in all, I had a nice pleasant day. Mum made us all a lovely tea, there was cake, biscuits, chocolates and a tasty dessert for afterwards which we all enjoyed.

Following that nice day, the winter loomed and it began to get cold. We would have foggy, damp, wet days and even colder nights. November up north was always cold, sometimes we would have a lot of snow, though not this year. I really felt the cold, when I was younger, I expect it was because I was very thin. Mandy however was chubby and plump. Puppy fat is what I thought and she would grow out of it in time.

Mum would still go out once a week to the dance club with her friends, Tony was still seeing Vickey, after all, they were engaged and due to marry the following year, in July. One night, Mum came home to find the house in full darkness, even the living room. Strange, she thought, where is Tony? He is supposed to be looking after the girls. As she approached the living room door, she heard someone giggle, scuffling about too and upon opening the door she was surprised to find Tony there with his shirt off and Vicky smoothing down her hair. Next thing, me and Mandy heard loud voices downstairs, it was Tony and Mum, just what had happened? Mum had told Tony off for not being respectful of her home and she asked him if Vickey would do the same in her parents' home. So after that, Vickey did not visit as much. Mandy was a little upset as she liked her. I agreed with Mum, not only that but us girls always had to go to bed earlier when she was here and that meant us missing our favourite programme on the television!

The winter soon came round again, bringing the cold, snow and ice. I was glad when the new year came, as Christmas was a bit dull that year. Simon did not visit, nor did Grandma and Grandad. We had a quiet one which was nice. The New Year brought the excitement of the forthcoming marriage in July of Tony and Vickey, however this time we were not to be bridesmaids. So from January onwards, there was a lot of planning to do, so we did not see much of Tony who was taking extra shifts with his job, so he could save up to put a deposit on a house for himself and Vickey.

March came, along with some lovely spring weather. It was mild, though warm some days and me and Mandy would play outside until 4 or 5 o'clock, sometimes over-tiring ourselves.

Well, as we approached the month of May, it was only 8 weeks or so to go before the wedding. Mum had decided what she would be wearing, me and Mandy were unsure. There were a few of the children off school poorly towards the end of May. One day, Mandy told me that she did not feel too good in herself. She had been scratching her head a lot for a few days and I began to notice that my head was itchy too. I thought to myself that perhaps it was nits, although we always used our own combs, so this did not add up. Mum became concerned, she began to check mine and Mandy's hair and scalp and after doing this, she decided to take us to the doctor, as she was unsure as to what the problem was. It turned out that we both had nasty infections of the scalp and needed a course of antibiotics to clear it up. We were given some special shampoo which smelt foul, we had to wash our hair with it every day for at least 2 weeks. In the meantime, both our scalps were very sore and painful. I did wonder if we had caught this from anyone at our school. Mum kept us both off school just in case it was infectious.

By the end of 2 – 3 weeks, it was soon to be Tony and Vickey's wedding, so Mum decided that me and Mandy would attend, but we had to cover our heads with a head scarf. We did, it did not look nice, but at least it meant that we could go. Three weeks passed quickly and it was now the day of their wedding, though neither of us was fully better so we could not enjoy the wedding as we would have done without our scalp problem. However, we did join in and we managed to have a little dance at the evening disco which was nice. Mum looked lovely as always, the bride was very radiant and Tony looked very handsome in his wedding suit; all in all, it was a great day. Me and Mandy were glad to get back home, soon we were into bed, it had been a long tiring day for us, as weddings always were. I never liked weddings, I do not know why. I still don't to this day.

That year, we had a beautiful hot sunny summer, a very long summer, we had lots of midges to cope with too and sometimes they were a nuisance. In August, Mum's boyfriend at the time suggested that we all go on the train to the nearest seaside resort, which we did and we all had a great day out, and the weather was lovely too. We all went again on the train in September and whilst we were there, we had fish and chips for tea, which was nice, and Mum managed to take a few photos of us. I did not like that part.

I would be 14 years old in 3 weeks, so I was looking forward to this birthday but it was around that time that my back began to cause me problems, in that it became very painful for me. The pain was high up my back, around my rib area. I did not tell Mum though, as I did not want to worry her, so I just decided to buy some pain tablets and analgesics from the local chemist. These eased the pain for a little while, though not all the time.

Mum bought me some lovely useful presents for my birthday. She made me a cake which was very sweet and tasty, though unlike Mandy, who loved any kind of cake, I was not too keen. I much preferred jelly and ice cream. Simon and Darren came with some gifts for me. Tony was too busy with his new house; Grandma and Grandad sent me some money, so I had a nice pleasant day.

A few weeks after this, the weather turned very cold again; we also had some damp days. The Christmas that year was very snowy, cold, and icy, a horrible one in fact. It even snowed on Christmas Day, so me and Mandy decided to wrap up to go outside and throw snowballs at each other. Sometimes we made a snowman, if we could get our hands warm enough to do so. Then, once again, the new year was upon us, which brought a lot of cold, rainy days, some hail thrown in too, though it waited until the end of February to snow and snow it did.

I was now having pains in my shoulder blades and various parts of my spine, every day. I continued with the painkillers right up to the start of June 1976, when I complained to my mum about it. She said that it was my school satchel which was too heavy for me. She suggested that she would collect me from school and carry it for me every day, which she did. In the meantime, the pain seemed to increase, not lessen, like I thought it would, and it went on for another 3 months or so. In the end, Mum felt that I needed to see our family doctor for his opinion. She would make me an appointment for the next week.

11

Back To Hospital

The following week, I took one day off school and we both headed to the doctor for his opinion as to what was causing me so much pain and discomfort. I knew that I had a problem with my spine as Mum had told me that my back was no longer as straight as it should have been. We went in to see our doctor who took one look at my back and he commented that he could not see what the problem was and that to him, my spine was straight, but Mum insisted on me having a second opinion as she was not convinced that my back was straight; she felt that there was something else going on, hence all the pain I was suffering with it.

Sadly, at this time in my life, due to my spinal problem, I became a target for the bullies at my school, who would call me nasty names. While I was waiting to see an orthopaedic surgeon for his diagnosis, the bullying continued. Up until this time I loved school, though the bullying continued relentlessly every day, so much so that I began to hate school, going there every day was a struggle for me. I became anxious, depressed and stressed; my sleep suffered, and my school work suffered, so, often I would bunk off school with one of my friends, I only had a couple at that time and we would go to her parent's house. Her parents worked so this was OK. I never told Mum about this, to this day she still does not know.

I gradually became more depressed, introverted, quiet in myself, not wanting to mix with anyone, not wanting to talk, so I decided to go to the local chemist to buy something to help me with all these feelings I was having, though it was mainly for the depression and anxiety. I bought some 'Quiet Life' tablets to help to calm me down. I would buy a few pots of these every week from my pocket money. However, in time I became very dependent on them; at that particular time, I was eating them like sweets.

One day Mum collected me from school, I was crying and when we got home, I told Mum all about the bullying I was receiving and how it was now affecting me. Well, she became very angry and she told me that she would go to see the headmaster about this, so he could punish the person who was responsible; it was mainly one boy who had been subjecting me to this barrage of nasty, hurtful, cruel comments.

The headmaster listened to Mum and he told her that he would speak to the boy as he did not condone any form of bullying at the school. This he did, he also advised Mum to have a word with the boy's parents to make them aware of the situation as he only lived on the next street. Mum went round one evening to speak to both his parents; his dad told Mum that they would punish him for this, and he thanked Mum for letting them know. From that time, the boy never bothered me again which I was pleased about.

My 15th birthday came and went. I had to wait 4-6 months for my appointment with the orthopaedic specialist, and the appointment came in February of 1977. Me and Mum travelled there on the bus to the hospital. I was quite nervous, not knowing what to expect, as I had never had any problems with my back up to this point. Both me and Mum went into the consulting room to be greeted by a rather stern, mature man, sitting at a desk. He greeted us as we sat down; Mum told him all about the pain in my back and how she thought my spine was curved. He asked me to take my top off and vest off, as I could not wear a bra, my back being too painful for me at that time. He examined my back and asked me to bend over to touch my toes, which I did, though it hurt me.

When I sat down again, he turned to face Mum and said that I had scoliosis. Mum asked what it was. He said, "It is another word for curvature of the spine." In my case, it was the upper part of my spine which was curved and this was the reason for all my pain and discomfort.

Well, me and Mum just looked disbelievingly at each other as we had never heard of this problem before. Then he suggested that he would refer me to an orthopaedic surgeon, who specialized in scoliosis and spinal problems; he would be able to advise me further and possibly suggest some treatment to help me. He stated that there was a 6-month waiting list just for the initial consultation, so we would have to be patient and wait for the appointment. In the meantime, I was advised to take some paracetamol for the pain and not to do anything too strenuous, which would aggravate my pain more.

The following 6 months, I continued to attend school, still taking the Quiet Life pills for my depression and anxiety. I felt that I could not put my mind on anything, the pain really got me down and the bullying began again, though it was not the same boy. I would still skip my lessons with my friend, sometimes twice a week. I really hated school, the pressure, stress, abuse and anxiety all got too much for me to take. I had my exams around that time, it was the GCSE's. I just could not concentrate on them with all of what was going on, hence the fact that I left school at 16 years old with not one GCSE to my name and no qualifications whatsoever.

In September of that year, I got my appointment to see the orthopaedic surgeon, this was around 3 weeks before my 16th birthday. As before, me and Mum went on the bus and I was feeling confident that this surgeon would be able to help me in some way. By this time, the pain in my back had increased and I was very tired every day. We entered the consulting room together to face a mature, very stern man. Mum once again explained why we were there. Then the surgeon asked me about my back and the pain, and when was it at its worst. To which I replied that it was bad now, every day, nothing seemed to touch it.

Once again, I was asked to take my top and vest off and to bend over to touch my toes, which I did, wincing as I straightened up. He examined my spine, touching all my vertebrae, especially the top one where the curvature was. He confirmed that yes, I did have scoliosis and that there was some treatment for it in the form of my being put on a bed with weights at the bottom of the bed which would in turn stretch my spine. If this did not help me, then the only other option he could offer me was a major operation involving a metal rod or rods being placed in my spine. This was, he stated, a preventative procedure as without anything being done, my curvature would undoubtedly in time become bigger and with it a host of other problems.

As I was nearly 16 years old, he felt that this operation had to be performed in the next 12 months as he had had a lot of success in correcting smaller curvatures like mine. He told me that the curvature was 52 degrees at that time. I was 5 foot 2 inches and very, very slim, which he said was good. The surgeon suggested that I try the traction first to see how I fared and if it decreased my curvature. He stated that as I was underage at the time for consent to this, it would be left for my mum to consider traction. She told him that it was up to me to decide as I was nearly 16 years old. So, we left the hospital with me having to make a huge decision about my future. This really scared me at this point, as a good part of my life up to then had been spent in hospital, seeing various specialists for my muscular dystrophy. So, we went home with me contemplating what was the best for me to do; should I have the traction? Well, I thought what would be the harm if I at least tried it?

We were both upset about this news regarding my back problems, I could not really consider an operation as I did not want to think about it, everything that the surgeon said just scared me. Around 2 months later, Mum took me to see our doctor as I had decided to try the traction. He told us that he would refer me and I would have to wait around 2 – 3 months to receive my appointment. As it turned out, I had to wait 6 months; I did receive my appointment for traction at the end of March. Mum had arranged transport through our doctor. We arrived at the hospital 20 minutes later, I was once again very anxious and nervous. She came with me again to the hospital, where we were greeted by a nurse who asked me to go into a cubicle to undress, put the hospital gown on and wait to be called, which I did.

I was shown to the X-ray department where a lot of photographs were taken of my spine, not by a machine but it was an actual photographer who just snapped away. I must have had a dozen photographs taken, some I had to bend over for, some to the right, some to the left. I was told to wait outside the room for all my photos and then to take them back to the nurse, which I did. Mum was there waiting for me in the waiting room, then the nurse said to me that I had to have a small marker inserted at the point of my curvature. She assured me that this procedure would not hurt me as it was only temporary.

Well, then I was shown to yet another room and asked once more to bend over, this was after the nurse had weighed me and taken my height. She asked me to bend over more to my left side, which I did and then I felt this sharp searing pain in my left shoulder blade area, directly on top of my curvature. I did not like the way it felt inside my skin. The nurse explained that it would only be in there for a few days and that I should have no problem lying on my back to sleep so this would be okay for me when having the traction. I made my way back to the original nurse who said that I could go home, I would receive an appointment for the traction; there would be 6, one-weekly appointments and after that, I would be seen by the orthopaedic surgeon again in the hope that the traction had helped to slow down my curvature.

So, I left the hospital with Mum, with all the contact details of that department and a feeling of utter dread came over me. Due to the marker under my skin, it made it so very difficult for me to lie on my back to sleep, as I was aware of it being there and I could feel it under my skin, it was not very nice.

One month later, I received my appointment to have my traction. Mum was there, I was told to lie down on a very narrow bed, weights were placed at the end of the bed and then the procedure began. I felt every pull on my spine and the marker became unbearable for me. I told the nurse this and she went away to ask the doctor on call for his advice. About 10 minutes later, she returned to tell me that the doctor thought it would be best for me not to have the traction as it caused me so much discomfort, being too much for me. He said that he would contact my orthopaedic surgeon to ask him if there was anything else that I could try. He told the nurse that I could go home and the hospital would be in touch with me, in that they would send me an appointment to see my orthopaedic surgeon. I was really pleased to be going home so soon. I just did not like the traction it was too painful for me. Me and Mum caught the bus back home. I felt a little disappointed and anxious at the same time, as to just what was going to happen to me next.

The following week, a letter arrived for me with an appointment to see my orthopaedic surgeon who unfortunately turned out to be the most arrogant, self-centred man, who made everyone around him nervous, even his staff, nurses, ward sisters and others who worked in the hospital; he had a reputation for this. So, as you can imagine, I was not looking forward to seeing him again.

The day came for me to see him, I felt very anxious and stressed about this, so I decided to take one Quiet Life tablet to calm me, which it did. Both me and Mum were shown into a small room; he marched in and said that as the traction could not be tolerated by me, the only other option was for me to have a major operation involving two metal rods inserted into the full length of my spine, after which I would be put on a 'stryker' bed. He explained that it was a very narrow bed and that every 4 hours I would be turned over from being on my back to being on my front. I had to stay on this bed following my operation for 3 to 4 weeks, after which I would be encased in a plaster of Paris pot, and whilst this dried, I would be put on a plaster bed to dry out, so it would allow the plaster of Paris to dry completely; this took around 1 week to 10 days.

The ward sister who came in the room with him told me that after this, I would be placed on a standing bed which would enable me to stand up for a while, then I was able to have a wash, brush my hair and eventually walk around. The whole time that I spent on the standing bed would depend on me, usually between

3 to 6 months. This procedure had to be done in stages and of course, monitored by the nursing staff. This would not be the end of my treatment though, as after this, I would be fitted with a corset, which was pulled in tight to support all of my spine. She said that I would have to wear the corset for 2 - 2½ years, day and night, except when I had a wash. I was allowed to take it off to have a strip wash.

So all in all, the time period for all this kind of treatment would be around 3 and a half years of my life, at the end of it, I would have a lovely straight spine, all the pain gone and able to do most things I wanted. Well, being 16½ years old at that time, 3½ years did not really seem a long time to me back then, so the ward sister suggested that I go home and think about it, as it was a huge decision for me to make; talk it through with my mum and family and then to give them a ring when I had made up my mind, as to what I wanted to do.

12

First Of Many

I had decided to go ahead with the surgery after everything had been explained to me that day. I told the surgeon that I did not need any time to think about it, as I felt being so young the time would soon pass, I just hoped that I would have the result I was looking for, though mainly I wanted the pain to go away. He was very pleased with my answer and replied that surgery would stop my curvature from getting worse later on. However, he stressed that the surgery came with a 50/50 chance of success, like most major operations did.

He told me that perhaps April would be the best month for him, that way I would be back home by October to celebrate my 17th birthday. As it was the end of March, it would not be long I thought before the operation would be performed. The day finally came, it was the end of April and I was to be admitted to the orthopaedic unit to have major surgery on my spine. My small travel bag was packed by lunchtime and as you can imagine, I was very anxious, nervous and apprehensive about things. Mum came with me as usual, she too was anxious and worried. When we arrived at the clinic, I was shown to my bed; a nurse came to check me in, she did all the things like weigh me, take a blood test, measure my height and then my name tag was fitted. She told me that my surgeon would come to see me later on, to go through the procedure and so on, as I was to have my operation the next day, the first in the morning.

When the tea trolley came around, both me and Mum were given one while we waited, waited and waited, at which point it was tea time for the patients. Then I heard his voice in the corridor. I began to feel anxious and nervous and to shake inside. I did not like these feelings which I suppose were normal under the circumstances. He came in with his entourage of nursing staff all in awe at the presence of this wonderful orthopaedic surgeon who thought too much of himself and his importance.

He explained that I would be the first on the list for surgery, my operation would be between 3 – 4 hours long and afterwards, I was to be brought back to the ward and placed on a Stryker bed, to begin the next stage of my treatment. He then asked me if I had any questions for him. As I was too scared, I just said no. When Mum began to speak to him, he just cut her off, turned his back on us and quickly walked away. Mum was like me, a bit annoyed about this attitude, he was just so arrogant and rude, I did not like his arrogant manner at all.

Mum stayed with me until 8 p.m. She left then to catch the bus back home. As the orthopaedic unit was around 10 miles from where we were living at that time, she had to get 2 buses to visit me each day which she did every day whilst I was in the unit; my stay there was about 5 to 6 months. After Mum left, I tried to settle down. Night came and I just could not get to sleep, I had too much on my mind.

The morning soon came around, and as I was nil to eat, I had 2 cups of tea and a glass of water, whilst I waited with anticipation. Around 9.30 a.m. the porter came for me with a gurney; a nurse was with him and she prepared me for surgery, giving me a hospital gown, plastic panties, and no jewellery was to be worn. Then the anaesthetist came to have a word with me; the gurney was wheeled in next to my bed, I was asked to get on it and then we were on our way to the theatre. We went into this rather small room where I was given the anaesthetic and told to count to ten. I managed to get to 6 and then nothing, until I was coming to in the recovery room. A nurse came to tell me that my operation went well, I started to move around as the bed seemed so narrow, it was then that I realised I was on the awful Stryker bed.

A few hours later, the surgeon came to see me. He was pleased, he told me how the operation went, also that I could go back to my ward the next day. Mum had already been to see me in the recovery ward. She came again the next day when I settled into the ward. Every 4 hours I had to be turned, 4 hours on our backs, 4 hours on our fronts; we had to eat like this, when we were over on our fronts we had a hole in the stryker bed which our heads went through, a drink was placed on a tray under the bed with a straw, our meals were put on this tray, it was an unusual way to eat, it took me a very long time to get used to it!

In time, I began to hate that Stryker bed, me and the other girls in my ward were on it for about 4 – 6 weeks. These girls were mostly teenagers like me, all going through the same procedure. I counted down the weeks, only 2 days to go I thought, not long now, by this time it was the middle of June, it was a nice, sunny month. Then 2 days later, the ward staff came for me around 11 a.m. and they took me to a big cool room down the long corridor. The ward sister was there waiting for me, as they wheeled in a standing bed. I was told not to be frightened as 2-3 nurses lifted me onto the standing bed, and then it began to tilt upwards and in no time I was standing up, though I did feel terribly dizzy, having been lying down for all those weeks.

The sister began to soak some cloth into the plaster of Paris and I was asked to stand very still which I did. The next thing I felt was some nice heat, a wrapping sensation as the sister began to wrap my body, shoulder to hip in this warm plaster of Paris, it seemed like an awful long time that I was standing as once again I began to feel quite faint, dizzy and tired. Then 2 – 3 minutes later, it was all over; I was put on the standing bed again, then transferred to the drying bed, which I had to stay on for 3 days until the plaster was fully dry. I was really glad to come off that drying bed, then the staff transferred me to my standing bed. It was like an armchair which you could raise up and down with a remote. Well, at least now I was in a ward with 4 other teenage girls, just like me, who had had the same or similar operation to me.

The next morning, the nurses came around with a bowl of water for each of us, so we had to gradually raise the bed until we were standing and then step away from our beds. The first time I did this I felt very faint and dizzy so I put myself back against the bed so that I would not fall over. Then slowly I made it to the bowl, to have a strip wash which was nice. After that I took my bed down, which was okay; in time I got used to this routine. When our meals came around, we had to either eat them on our sides or put the plates on top of the plaster pot. I managed to get used to this as well, though I still had to ask for a bedpan as at that stage, we were only standing and not walking. I never did like the bedpans, they were always so cold, though in time the hospital managed to get the plastic ones. I was on my standing bed for 4-6 weeks during which time Mum came to see me every day without fail. Mandy however, refused to come to see me, as she said that I was playing on my spinal problem, though I felt at the time that she was jealous of all the attention I was getting and she did not like it.

Simon, his wife, Tony and Vickey came to see me one day, though I could tell that they all felt very uncomfortable being there. Simon spent most of his time complaining about Mum and her new boyfriend; he just loved to moan about someone or something, he certainly was not a happy person. I never really enjoyed their visits, I would rather it be Mum. Sometimes Mum's friend came to see me, especially if Mum was not feeling too good in herself. I never did realise until later on, just how far the orthopaedic unit was from our home. It took Mum around 50 minutes on two buses every day to visit me. She would come to see me in the afternoon and stay there all day until 8 p.m., so as you can see, it was a very long day for her. Then, when she did go home, she would care for Mandy who was now 13 years old and had become very cheeky with Mum and with everyone. Whilst I was in hospital, she completely went off the rails, she was out of control most days. So, Mum did really have a lot on her plate. My 3 brothers did not help or support Mum in this, she really played Mum up.

One day in September, perhaps the beginning of October, the nurse came to see me to tell me that I had a visitor who would like to see me. Well, I thought that it might be Grandma or Grandad, but no, she said that it was my father, he was blind drunk, though he had some flowers for me. Well, as you can imagine, I was in shock, he had never bothered to get in touch with me before that, so I had never met him. I became very stressed and the ward nurse could see that I was upset. I told her that I did not want to see him, could she give the flowers to a patient, as I did not want them. At this point, I was really anxious and very annoyed at Dad for just turning up like that. I thought that he had a cheek, it was like the last 16 years of my life meant nothing to him.

However, what I did not realise was that a few days later, Simon had been to see Mum and he inferred that it was her fault that Dad could not visit me. Once again they had words; some shouting went on between them, though Mum was the only person ever to stand up to him, she was not afraid of him like everyone else was. Mum came to visit me the next day, and she apologised to me for Dad coming up to see me like that. We talked, I told her that the surgeon was doing his ward round soon and she said that she would stay with me, as she knew just how very nervous he made me feel.

Just before teatime he arrived and went to see all the girls in my ward and then he came to see me. He gave Mum a sharp look as if to say that she should not be on the ward. He said that as I was making fairly good progress, I would be going home soon, by the 1st of October at least, and then I was to have complete bed rest for 6 to 10 months. I was a little upset about having to go on bed rest, as I had spent so much time already lying down on my bed, but in those days, this was the norm, after having spinal surgery. Mum was very pleased to hear that I would be coming home at last, although she knew that I would need a bed downstairs, so she asked the social for a grant for me, which they gave her, and then it was time for her to go and look for a suitable orthopaedic bed for me which could be delivered around the end of September time. That day came for me at last, I was to leave the hospital, to go home, I could not wait to get back home again.

The transport arrived on time, an ambulance as I had to lie flat to travel. Mum had rung the ward to see what time I would be getting home, then before I knew it, we had arrived at our house. I was just so excited, however, Mum stood at the front door with a rather worried look on her face.

13

Back Home At Last

Mum told the ambulance men also me that my bed had not been delivered yet, so they placed me on the 3-piece suite we had in the lounge, whilst Mum frantically rang the shop about my bed, which did turn up around 1 hour later, to our relief. It was a lovely bed, I had a while to get used to it, this I did for the next 8 months. Mum had bought me a lot of games for me to play, these I enjoyed, also reading which whiled away the time.

A few friends whom I made at school did not visit me, I did not expect that they would, none of my brothers came to see me or support Mum through this most difficult, worrying time, so Mum had no form of support. Even my sister Mandy did nothing to help Mum, so now, looking back on my life, I do not have anything to thank my family for, it all fell to Mum to care for me 24 hours a day, 7 days a week. This she did every day, never complaining, just giving me her love, attention, support, also at the same time caring for Mandy.

The following 8 months soon went by, though around 4 days after my coming home, Mum received some terrible, sad news concerning my brother Darren, who was at sea on a trawler. Sadly, it had gone down with everyone on board, there were no survivors. It was a terrible tragedy. Mum was so upset, she arranged a memorial for Darren at home, a vicar came and said a few words which was nice.

At this point in our lives, our family was split apart by the betrayal of my 2 brothers, led by Simon, as they had arranged a memorial for Darren and my dad was there with his new lady friend, whom Simon had told the vicar taking the memorial that she was his and Tony's mother. Mum got to hear of this betrayal, which in a way was a form of abandonment by our two brothers, it was just awful at such a very sad time for all of us. When Mum told me and Mandy about this, I just could not understand how they both could do such a hurtful, cruel thing. So, from that day, 5th October 1978, both me and Mum have had no further contact with either of my brothers up to this day.

I was quite concerned about the next stage of my treatment, as it was now time for me to have my heavy plaster cast removed, as it did weigh one stone, it would be exchanged for some other form of support for my spine. I received my appointment for around the middle of May. The transport came and Mum was with me again; we arrived at the orthopaedic unit and the nursing sister came up to me and told me that I would be placed in a smaller, lighter pot, with zips at either side, which could be removed for me to have a wash. I liked this idea of having a lightweight pot, with the summer on the way, it would be easier for me to cope with. I was taken on a gurney into the plaster room and helped to stand by 2 nurses, then the sister once more began to wrap bandages soaked in a green liquid around my body, from my neck right down to my hips. It felt nice and warm as it was applied; when finished, as before, I was placed on the drying bed for 3 days after which I was given a standing bed, like before. Only now I knew the routine; this time I did not feel as dizzy as I did the first time around.

This pot was certainly lighter, after a few weeks I was shown how to take it off, so I could wash my chest, stomach etc. This time, I was on a standing bed for 6 – 8 weeks in all, after which I had to see an occupational therapist to practise going up and down the stairs as we lived in a house. I had to practice doing this, as it was all about me gaining confidence, which I never did have much of anyway.

After being in the hospital for around twelve weeks, the surgeon made his rounds one day and told me that I was to be discharged in 2 days' time, so I was going home again. I was really very happy about this. I told Mum when she came to visit me later on in the day. She like me was pleased, though apprehensive at the same time. The hospital arranged my transport, of course, it was an ambulance as once again, I had to lie down for travel. I was unable to travel in a car, on a bus or on a train. The only way that I could travel was by an ambulance. So I arrived home in the ambulance, it was just great to get away from hospital, the ward, the nurses and staff, and everyone there in fact.

Mum made me a nice cup of tea, we had a little chat, my bed was still made up in the lounge. I also had another one upstairs, so the aim in time was for me to gradually use the stairs. The very first time I attempted this, I felt very strange doing it, I did not really like the way it made me feel. I felt shaky, uneasy and unbalanced the first two or three times, though after this I was okay. On the sixth day of being home, I managed to get right to the top of the stairs. I went into my bedroom which Mum had decorated herself for me, whilst I was in hospital, it was lovely. Then that night, for the first time in ages, I slept on my original bed, oh it felt so good. For the next 2 to 3 weeks I slept in late most days as I had been unable to get much sleep on the ward, what with everything going on.

That year, the spring was mild, the summer was quite hot and we had a lot of flies and midges about, so this lighter-weight pot was much cooler for me, which was great. I had to wear it for 6 months or so, I still had to rest for 2 hours a day. I was encouraged to walk as an exercise, so me and Mum would go for a walk, mainly at nighttime, that way not many people could see me as I still had no confidence in myself whatsoever. It was Mum who encouraged me to go out, I was not confident enough to do this in the day.

The first time Mum helped me to take my pot off, to have a strip wash, I felt quite faint, dizzy and weak in myself, however, I did not faint. In time this gradually eased, until when I took it off I could wash myself without any help, it was great to be able to wash once again. My pot did press on my chest, it had to be fairly tight to support my spine. One day I felt very congested, so much so that I could not breathe and my chest really hurt. Mum was very concerned about this, so she called the doctor, who came to see me. He diagnosed a chest infection, he stated that as my pot was so tight this did not help me, he advised Mum to contact the hospital to see if they could help me in some way.

The hospital arranged for an ambulance to collect me from home to take me to the orthopaedic unit, which they did. The ward sister met me and I was rushed into a side room. She looked at my pot and suggested that I needed an opening to be made in it, around my chest area. The next thing I knew a man had entered the room, with what looked like a chainsaw, only smaller. He came towards me with it and in no time at all I had a nice-sized hole in my pot, this would enable my chest to feel a lot easier, and also my chest infection, which in time it did. I returned home after this was done, it was a lot better, cooler too for me and my chest infection cleared up, by which time we were into the summer. I would often sit outside to get some of the sun, then before I knew it, it was time for me to have my pot removed which was now to be replaced with a stiff corset, as a support for my spine.

I was quite apprehensive about this last leg of my operational procedure as I had to be measured up for a corset which had 2 metal rods in the back, for support for my spine and whalebone in the front of it which had to be laced up quite tightly. I was informed by the surgeon that I had to wear this for 24 hours a day, even when I slept and only to remove it to have a wash. So once again, Mum helped me with this, when it was time for it to be released and undone, so I could wash. The first time that Mum unlaced my corset for me, I felt so funny, strange and faint once more, the weakness came back again. Mum advised me to lie back down on the bed until the faintness subsided, which it did. I then had a little wash, though felt very weak and vulnerable without my support. Mum tightened it once more for me. I then sat down on my high-backed chair, which Mum had bought for me. However, it was not pleasant to sit down in my corset, as it dug into me.

I had to wear this for around 18 months during which time I was not allowed to use any form of public transport, so I was very restricted from going away etc. Mum suggested that we would have a little break away at the seaside, the nearest beach being around 30 miles away, so Mum arranged for an ambulance to transport me. I managed to take my own mattress; we stayed in a nice hotel for the weekend and I really enjoyed my break away, as did Mum, it made a change for her too, not having to do any cooking. It did us both a world of good, I must admit it was very unusual to travel by ambulance, though it got us there, and that was all that mattered at the time. Mandy went to stay with Mum's friend, whilst we were away, so Mum did not have to worry about her.

That year was fairly hot, with the summer once again being muggy with very hot, dry days. I really felt it whilst wearing my corset! We had a later summer that year, from the end of July onwards, August, September and parts of October were very warm, hot, and humid with lots of midges around too. The summer just flew by that year. I had then gotten used to wearing my corset. Once again me and Mum had a small break in October to the seaside. After we returned, Mum asked me if I would be alright to travel to Amsterdam in Holland the following year. I said that I would love to visit Holland!

Christmas came along, and again with it the snow, ice and frost. I was unable to go out in it. Mum and Mandy did though and we had a quiet time with no word from either Simon or Tony. I was pleased that Simon no longer came to visit us, though it would have been so nice to see Tony again.

The New Year arrived, it was now 1980, and this was the year that Mum would meet her second husband, Jerry, on her birthday that year. January and February were both cold months, March came around, with very cold winds and a little rain, though we did have a few mild days. At that time, Mum had been my full-time carer for around 2 years, her female friend suggested that she could do with a really good night out, being stuck in with me for 2 years. She deserved to have a night out and Mum's friend said that she would look after me for one evening. Mum was not sure about this, as all of her confidence had gone, being in so long. However, she arranged to go to a singles club where her female friend said that she would meet her and buy her a birthday drink to celebrate, so at least she did not have go to into the club on her own.

So that evening, after Mum's friend came to look after me, she caught the bus and off she went, feeling very nervous and apprehensive about this night out. Her friend met her off the bus and they went in together.

14

Changes

Jerry was in the corner of the room playing on a slot machine, Mum and her friend went up to the bar to get a drink. As Mum was tee-total, she had a small sherry to celebrate her birthday. Most times Mum only ever had a sherry at Christmas or on her birthday. As they were on their way back from the bar, Jerry came over to them and asked if he could join them as it was his first time at the singles club too.

He stayed with Mum all the time and after having quite a few dances together, he asked her if he could escort her to the bus at the end of the evening, which he did. They exchanged telephone numbers and no sooner had Mum arrived home, than the phone rang. It was Jerry, he must have been keen. So, I guess that Mum had left an impression on him. He was very keen alright, little did we know back then.

Mum began to see Jerry who was around 17 years older than her, on a regular basis. He did all the chasing around after Mum, she seemed to enjoy his company. When they went out, Mum's friend would keep an eye on me just in case I needed anything. Mandy at that time was never in, she went out most nights with her friends, she went out mainly to avoid me as we never saw eye to eye, we were like chalk and cheese, having nothing in common. Mum had been going out with Jerry for around 10 months, when one evening, he asked her to marry him. Mum went to his flat to celebrate, then the next day she told me and Mandy the good news. I could see that Mum was really happy and excited about getting married again as at that time, she had been on her own for around 18 years since divorcing my dad.

Neither me nor Mandy welcomed the idea of this massive change in all our lives, as even then for some reason, we both did not like him. Way before they were married, he showed some strange, unusual ways. He did some strange things, often he was very moody and silent for days, you could not get anything out of him, he was so deep, there definitely was something wrong with him.

The wedding was set for the following year in the summer. By that time, I would be out of my lightweight pot and supposedly on the right track to recovery. Gradually with Mum's help, I could climb the stairs, in time completely unaided which was good. I was now able to travel on public transport, though I did not have the confidence to do so at first, I would walk to most places, with Mum of course, we would often have a walk at night, especially in the summer.

The summer that year was quite lovely and it was great for me to get out and about once again, having been confined to the house for so long. The autumn came so soon, though it was mild. I had to go back to the hospital for my 6 monthly check-up. My surgeon was pleased with my progress and so was I at that time. I asked him if I could go away the following year and he said that there was no reason why I could not.

By this time, my 18th birthday had come and gone and winter was fast approaching. It was a very cold one, Mum would not let me go out in it, only to appointments of course, this was to protect me in case I fell on the ice. Then Christmas arrived and neither of my 2 brothers came to visit us, so they never got to meet Jerry. Just as well I thought, knowing Simon he would have pulled him to bits, just like he had done with most of Mum's previous boyfriends. I welcomed the new year of 1980, as I was feeling a lot stronger in myself, I had put on some weight which was good for me.

In February, Mum suggested that we should go shopping for her wedding outfit, in particular her dress, as they were getting married at the Registry office. Mum had a nice birthday that year, Jerry took her out for a meal to celebrate the fact that they had known each other for one year. The wedding was set for the end of May; this was good as May is a nice month, not too hot and not too cold.

Mum had booked us a long weekend away at the end of March to go to Holland on the ferry, which we did, just me and Mum. We had a lovely time, it was quite tiring for me some days though, Mum did enjoy it too. When we returned, Mum concentrated on the wedding plans, there were to be 30 guests, mostly her friends and neighbours. Jerry had around 4 or 5 guests; he was not very popular at work and none of his family had been invited either.

Me and Mandy went with Mum to choose her wedding dress; she opted for a lovely floral pink dress with matching shoes and handbag. We had bought her and Jerry a useful wedding gift. I had a few clothes at that time, Mandy however did not. Unlike me, she would go through tops, skirts and dresses like I do not know what. So Mum took her to the shops in town one day to buy something suitable, which she had to keep for the wedding.

Then Mum's big day arrived and we all went in the morning for our hair appointments. Mum was a bag of nerves and very anxious at the same time. We all made our way to the Registry office in town; it was a warm, pleasant day. Mandy became annoying, pulling at her pretty cotton dress. Mum looked beautiful, radiant and very happy. I could not help feeling sad for her though, as I felt that there was more to Jerry than met the eye. I had seen a little of it when they became engaged, though I could not put my finger on what it was, however, I do know that he was jealous of me and Mandy. In a way at that time, I felt that I was losing a part of Mum as it had been just us 3 for quite a long time. We would all have to adapt, I guess, once they were married.

The ceremony was short and sweet and afterwards, we all went to a local pub, to celebrate the happy couple. Throughout that time a few of Mum's friends had gone home and Jerry only had one friend left. Mum told me to keep an eye on Mandy as she had a liking for any kind of alcoholic drink, whereas me and Mum hardly touched it, except at weddings, Christmas etc. just to be sociable. Mandy had managed to have a few sneaky drinks and quite a lot of food too. I found her outside the pub, she was a little tipsy, so was given a lot of coffee to drink. Mum was very sober, as was Jerry. After around 3 hours all the guests had left, Mandy had now sobered up and we all made our way home in a taxi. It had been a very tiring day.

As Mum and Jerry were leaving to go on their honeymoon, as we arrived home, Mum's friend was there waiting for us. Their cases were all packed and they were on their way for one week's honeymoon, once they had both changed into their attire. Me, Mandy, Mum's friend Sandra and her daughter waved them off in Jerry's car, which had been decorated for the occasion. A dread suddenly came over me, I now had the job of keeping Mandy under control, it was my sole responsibility to look after her, making sure she attended school, did her homework and did not get into any trouble. A very difficult task lay ahead of me, one which I was not looking forward to.

Unfortunately for me, I did not do a good job of taking care of Mandy as for the whole week I never saw anything of her. She went out with her friends and when I did see her, I just got a lot of sarcastic remarks and replies from her. She really was very cheeky to me, I knew now how Mum must have felt when I had been in hospital.

We did not take to Mum's new husband, Jerry. Mandy more so, he seemed a strange, odd man with unusual ways, I guess it was his age, as he was a lot older than Mum. She rang us every day, which Jerry did not like or agree with. I know I should not have, but I did complain to her a little bit about Mandy and her antics. I did miss Mum; after all, it was only the second time that she had left us to go away, being just the 3 of us. It did feel rather alien having to adapt to someone else living with us.

That week went by very quickly, though upon arriving home, Mum did not get the reception from us that she was expecting, as me and Mandy had had a big argument that day and the atmosphere was very tense. I realise now that being the eldest, I should have made more of an effort to make both of them welcome. I should at least have acknowledged them. I feel around this time my depression had set in with me, I had left school with no qualifications, straight into having spinal surgery and all that it entailed, at that time I felt that my life was in limbo, I had no goals, I really did not know what to do with myself.

15

Mum at that time had a little canvassing job and she suggested that perhaps I would like to do something similar; so she had a word with her boss. Like Mum I was given a round not far from our home, it would get me out of the house, meeting new people. "Who knows," she said to me, "you may even make some friends?"

Around 4 weeks later, this is what I did. Mum showed me the basics of what to do, leave the brochure with the customer and collect it in a week or two. So at least this little job would give me something to occupy myself with as most of the time I was moping about at home, getting up late, going to bed late, and going out for a walk when it was nice in the day. At that time, I seemed to not have much motivation in myself as my self-confidence was very poor; I was never confident anyway. Perhaps my operation and hospital stay had not helped me in that respect.

After Mum and Jerry had been married for around 11 months or so, Jerry suggested that we should all go away on holiday together. He had a friend who owned a caravan at the seaside. So, it would not cost us much, only our spending and food costs. Both me and Mandy were very excited about going away, one week of sun and sand. Mum was pleased too, though she did not fancy all the cooking and cleaning, still, it made a change for her.

Just after the Easter break, we all set off in Jerry's car for our lovely break away. Little did we know back then what lay in store for us and how Jerry would really show us his true colours. In time, this would become a life-changing event for poor Mum as she would realise just what a very big mistake she had made.

We arrived at the caravan site late afternoon on a Saturday. The caravan was rather pokey, to say the least, though me and Mandy did have our own bedroom which was good. There were all the kitchen utensils, pans and such and the site was quite large, it had a café, bar, club, toilets, communal showers and was full of family members, very busy indeed. Mandy went out on her own to check it out for herself. Really, she just went out to see if there were any available good-looking boys hanging around.

Jerry and Mum went to a nearby shop to stock up on food and essentials. That evening we all had a nice cooked tea which Mum made. As we were all going out that night, Mum looked very pretty in her summer dress. Mandy was ages in the bathroom, as she always was, she told Mum that she was going for a walk to get some air. Mum suggested that I go with her, which I did, though I did not want to as I knew exactly what she had on her mind.

However, she surprised me that night as we did just go for a walk around the area. We came to the entertainment club and listened to the music outside, before we knew it, it was nine o'clock, time to head back to the caravan as Mum had told me that she wanted Mandy home by 9.30 pm. We were both tired that night with all the travelling, we looked forward to what the next day would bring.

The following day Jerry took us to the next seaside town. We had some lunch and Jerry suggested we all have a game on the gaming machines, so Mum changed around 50 pence and gave us each 25p in coins to put in the machine. I did not mind the machines, Mum was not too keen on them and neither was Mandy. Afterwards, we all went for a stroll along the promenade. Mum said that she would like to eat at the café in the caravan site that night, she said that the meals looked nice, so Jerry agreed and we set off for home.

We had a lovely tasty meal at the restaurant, well, bar-café as it was, and as we were leaving, Mum heard some music and wondered what it could be. She suggested that we should all go and see; it was a sort of family cabaret night at the club there and it was rather packed. Jerry found us a table and went to order us some drinks. Mandy went with him to help, she asked for a shandy and was told that she was too young to have a shandy or any alcoholic drink. Upon returning from the bar, both me and Mandy noticed a man on his own who had his eyes fixed on Mum. He seemed rather pleasant enough, he acknowledged all of us when we got up to leave, as the club closed at 11.30 p.m. Jerry did not seem to like the way that the man was admiring Mum. Anyway, the next thing on the way back to the caravan, they started to argue. Me and Mandy put our eyes up in the air, trust Jerry to start things I thought, after we had had a really nice day. The argument continued, and as we arrived back at the caravan we went straight to bed, though I could still hear them shouting. Then there was a loud bang as the door to the caravan shut. I could hear Mum crying; I guessed that Jerry had gone out to cool down.

The next day at breakfast, the atmosphere was very frosty as Mum and Jerry were not talking to each other, they were just giving each other dirty looks, neither of them having had much sleep. After breakfast, Jerry cleared off in his car, telling us that he was just going for a ride. Me, Mum and Mandy went out for a walk around the resort, along the promenade. We had lunch at one of the cafes there, we went on the beach, had a nice relaxing day and when we arrived back at the caravan, we found Jerry there, he said that he wanted to talk to Mum so they went into their bedroom for some privacy.

Jerry said that he would make the tea that night as he and Mum would be going for a drive that night. After tea, they set off in Jerry's car around 7 p.m. Me and Mandy decided to go to the club on the site, there was some entertainment on, a group and then a magician. As I was old enough, I went to the bar to buy Mandy an orange juice. I had a coke as I did not like alcohol, anyway on my way back from the bar, the same man who had been looking at Mum the previous night was there. He acknowledged both me and Mandy and asked if he could join us at our table, I said yes.

He started asking me about Mum, as to where she was that evening. I said that she had gone out with her husband, and then after a while, he asked if he could buy us a drink. I had a coke, Mandy another orange juice, though she would have preferred a shandy, she was too young to drink. We stayed at the club for about 3 hours during which time Mandy noticed some young lads hanging around outside, so as we went to go, the man said to tell Mum hello and he hoped that he would see her again sometime, to which I replied under my breath, "Blooming cheek, she is a newly married woman."

Mandy started chatting to the 3 lads who said that they were going to take a walk along the beach. I did not like this idea, I told them that Mandy could not go with them, she had to come home with me. I tried everything to encourage Mandy to come back with me, though in true Mandy style, she was not having any of it. So I shouted back at her not to be too late, as she continued walking on in the company of the 3 lads. I realised after they had gone out of sight that I should have gone with her, being so young, as anything could happen to her. I got back around 11.30 p.m., had a cup of tea and went to bed.

Mum and Jerry returned around 12.30 a.m. and once again they were arguing and shouting at each other. Mandy returned about 1 a.m. She sneaked in through the front door and made a run for her bedroom upon which Mum came out of her bedroom and asked where she had been till this time.

"Just out," Mandy said.

Mum replied, "I will speak to you tomorrow about this, now get to bed!"

The next day was a beautiful, sunny day, there was once again not much conversation at the breakfast table, though Mum did tell me off for not seeing Mandy home earlier. I just shrugged and said, "Well you know what she's like."

That day me and Mandy went to the nearby park and left them both to sort things out. We got back in time for tea which was fish and chips. We all sat at the table, no one saying much. I told Mum that last evening, the gentleman on his own had asked about her and that he bought us a soft drink. Mum nodded and said that was nice. Jerry glowered at her, he was jealous, you could tell. After tea, me and Mandy watched some television, then we got ready to go to the club as tonight; there was a talent show on which seemed quite interesting.

We told Mum this and she said if we waited an hour or so, she would come with us as Jerry was in a bad mood.

So, she went to get ready, she asked both of us to come into the bedroom with her, as she was so scared of Jerry. He returned around 10 minutes later and started banging on the bedroom door, saying that he was not letting Mum out to meet some man, as she was his wife. As the bedroom door locked from the inside, he started to force his way into the room. We were all frightened so Mum asked Mandy to climb out the bedroom window and go and ring the police to tell them that she was being threatened by her husband who would not let her go out.

So, off Mandy went, she climbed out of the window and ran all the way to the nearest phone box on the site. She returned a few minutes later as we heard a police car draw up. Two policemen entered the caravan, and upon hearing the police, Jerry scarpered. Mum explained the situation to the police officers and they both advised Mum to get a divorce from Jerry, to which Mum replied,

"What do you mean? We have only been married 11 months."

They advised Mum to contact a solicitor when she returned home, this was to arrange divorce proceedings as Jerry's jealousy and behaviour would only worsen in time, and as they said, "Who knew just what he would be capable of." This was an awful situation for all of us, so Mum suggested that me and Mandy should sleep in the same room as her, that way we would all be together. She feared for us, especially as Jerry was in such a foul mood and very, very unpredictable.

He came back around 1 a.m. and started knocking on the bedroom door.

Mum shouted, "Go away, just leave me alone."

Anyway, the knocking went on throughout the night at various times and at around 6 a.m. he turned the hoover on and hoovered around the caravan, anything to make a noise, also to make sure that none of us had any sleep. In between this, he put the radio on full blast, aggravating, annoying man that he was, how people change I thought.

The next thing we knew, the electrics had gone, so Jerry went to get some coins for it. When he left, we all got up, Mum said to pack our cases as quickly as possible, as we were going home. She had had enough of his jealous antics, our lovely break away had been ruined by his jealousy and threatening behaviour.

He came back 20 minutes later, shouting at Mum, "Where are you going?"

"Home," she said. "You'd better not stop us either as the police know everything, you will be getting a visit from them I expect, they did say that they would be back today to speak to you."

At that precise moment, we all heard a police car siren as 2 police cars pulled up outside the caravan. Mum went out to speak to them, then the next thing we were all bundled into their car, and as we left, Jerry was at the caravan being cautioned by the police. They took us to the nearest train station, upon which we caught the next train back home. What an awful holiday this had been for us all, I really did feel sorry for Mum.

16

More Changes To Come

When I did get back home, I began to have awful shooting pains at the top of my spine where the two Harrington rods had been placed. As time went on the pain became unbearable for me, so much so that it hurt to lie down on my spine. I told my mum about it and our doctor was called. He gave me a home visit. After examining me, he said that the wound was infected and yes, both rods had begun to protrude out of my spine. This was the reason for my pain. He advised me to go to see my orthopaedic surgeon as soon as possible. I received an appointment for 7 weeks' time. The doctor suggested that I sleep on my side. Mum was advised to dress my wound every day. I was given antibiotics for the infection as Mum was so worried about me, she suggested that she sleep in my bedroom on the floor near to my bed, so she could keep an eye on me, in case I needed anything in the night. Jerry who was still living with us, was not keen on this idea, as you can imagine in the days that followed, he made this very, very clear to us. They had been married at that time around 15 months during which time Mandy had been inquiring about her dad, she was now 16 years old, having just had her birthday.

She began to stay out late at night, playing Mum up something terrible, and teasing and annoying Jerry every chance she got, she made sure that he knew that she did not like him. The situation at home became unbearable for poor Mum, she was so torn. She had me to care for, Mandy being so uncontrollable and Jerry becoming more nasty and annoying as the days passed. Looking back, it must have been a very stressful difficult time for Mum, though she never complained about her lot in life. In the end, Mum arranged for Mandy to go and live with her dad, his wife and 2 step sisters. Mandy was really excited about meeting her dad as he came to collect her from our house. So that left Mum, me and Jerry.

Before I knew it the day arrived for me to see my orthopaedic surgeon, who as always made me nervous and anxious. He took one look at my back and said, "My goodness, how long has it been like this?"

He told me that I would be admitted into the orthopaedic unit in 1 week's time to have both troublesome rods removed. So, the next week me and Mum arrived at the hospital, early in the morning. I was to be in the unit for 2 days. Mum left and I went down to the theatre, around lunchtime. It took about 20 minutes to remove both of the rods, and then I was taken back to the ward and was told that I could now go to have a wash, walk to the toilet, and even get dressed if I wanted. At first, I felt so weak in myself, though later on I did go to have a wash and use the toilet. It felt rather strange not having the support there in my spine. The very next day the transport came to take me home. The nurse said that in 6 weeks' time my surgeon would like to see me on a follow-up appointment, so as soon as I got home, I made an appointment. Mum was very pleased to see me, Jerry not so.

The 6 weeks went by quickly and we found ourselves at the hospital again. My surgeon looked at the wound which had healed very nicely, and then he turned to me and said that I would have to wear a halo, which would stretch my spine to enable 2 more Harrington rods to be put back into my spine. I found the idea of wearing a halo fixed to my head and hips repulsive. I did not fancy having it done, he could see that I was hesitant about it and stated abruptly that if I did not consent to this procedure, there was nothing more he could do for me, I would just have to go home. His mannerism was so disgusting, he really gave me no choice.

As he put me on the spot to make a decision there and then, I agreed to have this procedure. Being 20 years old at that time, I really wanted to get myself better, well again and not have to suffer more pain in my spine and hips. Mum put her eyes up in the air as he stormed out of the room once again. I began to tremble inside at the thought of wearing such a thing. I had around 9 months to wait for my operation, one of many at that time. The situation was very tense, as Mum had to go to court to get a restraining order taken out on Jerry to leave the house. Whilst we were both at the court that day, he took all of the furniture and everything they had bought for the wedding; he moved it all and hid it. He stole it from Mum and sadly she never saw any of it again.

When we returned from the court, our house looked like a tip, most of the furniture was gone. We were both very upset as we cleared around and tidied up. I really felt for Mum, what Jerry and Mandy put her through, and also me with all my health problems. Looking back though, she had been my rock. I will always be grateful to her for being there for me as not one of my other family members was. Mum was very loyal and supported me in every way possible. She believed in me, good job she did!

My operation was booked for the following September, just before my 21st birthday which I would have to celebrate in hospital.

17

Following that awful day when Jerry robbed Mum, she contacted her solicitor regarding this. However, as no one could locate him, Mum never got any of her furniture back. She began to concentrate more on her part-time job, canvassing, like I did. We would go out together and then after going on different roads, make our way home. I did enjoy meeting new people at that time, though my back once again was becoming more painful for me.

In September of 1982, I received my long-awaited appointment for my operation which was in 2 days' time. We made our way to the orthopaedic clinic and within 30 minutes, I was taken down to the theatre, they gave me a general anaesthetic to put me under. When I came round, I had a violent headache, I felt sick, the halo was there right in my face as you say, I hated it, straight away. I had to wear it for 7 weeks during which time the nurses would come every day to move the rings on it upwards; this would stretch my spine a little day by day.

The halo was so bulky and very, very wide so Mum had some skirts made for me which I could pull over my head to get on and she bought me some loose dresses which were comfortable to wear. I sat propped up by pillows in bed to sleep as once again, I could not sleep on my back. Mum visited me every day. Those weeks dragged by for me, at the end of the 7 weeks, the nurse measured my height; I had been stretched around 3 inches.

Then the orthopaedic surgeon came to see me, to inform me what would happen next. The procedure was that they would remove my halo in the theatre and I would have 2 more rods placed in my spine; at the same time, I was to have a bone graft fixed to my spinal discs, this was to strengthen my spine, the bone being taken from my left leg. This was to be a huge operation, taking between 5-6 hours. I was assured by him that this would benefit me and help me to lead a more normal life. He was very confident and hopeful, I, on the other hand, was unsure. Two surgeons operated on me, one to take the bone from my leg, and the other one had to go through my side to place both Harrington rods into my spinal cavity. I remember coming to whilst in the theatre, hearing all the noise, then there was nothing, I was out for the count.

When I did come around, I was on the dreaded Stryker bed again with the same old routine as before, 4 hours on my front, 4 hours on my back. Oh! How I disliked that bed! My surgeon came to see me in the recovery ward to tell me that my operation went well and the bone graft too. After being on the Stryker bed, I had the same procedure to look forward to, the plaster of Paris pot would be placed on my body again, only this time it would not weigh one stone, it would be a lot lighter. It would be made of a lighter plaster and have zips on either side. Then I was to be put on the drying bed for a few days and then transferred to the standard bed, to begin my rehabilitation, as it were. All of this was to take around 4 – 6 months, possibly longer depending on how I progressed. As stated earlier, I celebrated my 21st birthday in hospital, my mum bought me a lovely cake and some beautiful flowers. All the girls in my ward shared the cake which was so nice.

Altogether, it would take a further 7 months before I was strong enough to go home. Was I glad about this, glad to be going home again, glad to see the back of that place! Mum had arranged for my bed to be placed in the lounge. It was now the middle of March and the light pot was to be worn for another few weeks, then it would be removed, upon which I would be fitted up for a brace, not a corset as before. The brace would have 2 metal bars down the back and front for support and tied up in the front like a very tight corset. I was allowed to undo it, to take it off for me to have a bed bath, which Mum was instructed to do for me. The first time she did, I felt really faint and dizzy, so it had to be put back on again. Bed rest was to be the norm for me, I was to wear this brace for 12 – 18 months.

The summer of 1983 was quite warm, so wearing the brace was very uncomfortable for me. After I had worn it for 6 months, I was due to see my surgeon again. My transport was arranged, once again a lying-down ambulance. Mum came with me back home again and into the same routine, only this time it was just me and Mum as Mandy was now living at her dad's house and Jerry had found somewhere else to live.

Time moved on and before I knew it, I had just 6 months before the brace would be removed for good. Sadly for me, the same pain I had previously started again at the top of my spine. Once more it became unpleasant for me to lie on my back, only this time I was able to go up the stairs to bed. Mum became anxious and worried for me and again, she rang our doctor and was told that the district nurse would call to see me the next day, to take a look at my back, which she did. She told us that it seemed both of the rods were protruding at the top of my spine; she placed a dressing on the wound and advised me once again to sleep on my side, which I did though this time it was not for 7 – 8 weeks. Mum rang the hospital to inform them of this, they said they would send me an appointment for 4 weeks' time, to see my surgeon. In the meantime, Mum was to dress my wound to keep it clean, which she did.

Looking back, Mum had a lot of responsibility to care for me, she being my sole carer. The 4 week wait soon passed and I was sent to the hospital by ambulance. My surgeon took one look at my spine and said,

"Oh no, not again. Well, I'm afraid that both rods will need to be removed; this will be done tomorrow. You should be able to go home in a few days, then I would like to see you in the outpatients' department in 6 weeks."

At that point, I felt very discouraged and disappointed. Mum too looked a little down and forlorn, though she did stay with me that day until teatime.

The very next day in the morning, I was prepped for theatre. Around one hour later, I was up in the recovery ward, feeling rather sore. I did not really feel like moving about too much, so I rested for a while; once again it felt strange no brace, no support for my back, I felt really light. I decided to go to the toilet and have a wash, which I did, albeit shakily and unsteady in myself. I came back to my bed and asked the nurse for some pain relief as it was now beginning to hurt. I did manage to get some sleep that night. The next day my surgeon came to see me and told me I could go home the next day which was great. At this point, it seemed the ward and hospital were becoming my second home after spending more time there than at our home itself.

18

Holiday Time

When I did arrive back home, Mum suggested that a nice little break away would be good for us both; this was to be the following March as she had seen a good tour to Amsterdam in Holland. We would travel on the ferry over there and stay in a hotel for 5 nights; it really did sound exciting. At least by March time, I would be feeling stronger in myself. We were now approaching another winter which, living in the north of England, was never pleasant. Christmas came and went that year, with just me and Mum, a quiet time for us. It was so good for me to spend it at home instead of in hospital like in other years. I received an appointment at the beginning of March to see my surgeon, just for a check-up. I did hope though that this would be the last time I had to see him.

Then March followed by spring came around. As both me and Mum boarded the ferry, I thought to myself that at last, I might start to get back to some form of normality in my life. We did not like the ferry, neither of us was a good sailor, we were so pleased when we did eventually dock in Holland. We boarded our coach to take us to our hotel in Amsterdam. This was my very first holiday abroad, I was so excited about it, as was Mum. Once at the hotel, we were shown to our room which was light, spacious and airy. After having changed our clothes, we went down for our dinner. I wondered what would become of our break away and anticipated the next 4 days with relish.

We really made the most of our time away as there was so much to see and do. One of my favourite memories was going to visit Anne Frank's house; how tiny and cramped it was, I was left in wonder, how all those people lived there. That day we both returned home happy and tired, I was so glad to get back to my comfortable hotel bed.

This would be the first of many holidays me and Mum went on. However, for me, I was so proud that I had actually managed it. Summer that year was quite warm; my hospital appointment was for the end of the year, around November time and as it was just for a check-up, we would not be too long at the hospital.

Mum came with me once again and we were shown into a small cubicle. My surgeon came in so full of self-assurance and surety. He examined my spine, once again, then turned to tell me that he was sorry but there was not much more that he could do for me and I was discharged from his care. Well, I looked at him in disbelief, as did Mum. Before we knew it, he had gone. All thoughts started running through my mind; my spine at that time was still very curved, in time it would get worse, so how could he just leave me like this? As we left the cubicle, a young man around my age came from the cubicle next door; his scoliosis was even worse than mine, like me he was told the same.

We both arrived home rather disappointed and upset about my surgeon's nonchalant, could-not-care-less attitude, neither of us really wanted to talk about things that night, so we decided to watch a film on the television to take our minds off the awful disappointing, upsetting day we had.

So now, what was I going to do with myself? I asked myself, as I had no job, though Mum did have a part-time job selling tights to the neighbours; also she had a large round with quite a few customers in the area. So, she suggested to me that I start the same job and that I would canvas in what she called the posh area of the estate we lived in. She was sure that in time I would build up my own round. This is what I did for the next 8 months or so. I really enjoyed meeting different people and getting out of the house, it really gave me an interest and purpose, which was positive for me. During my bone graph operation on my spine, I got to meet the cardiothoracic surgeon who had assisted my surgeon who had operated on my spine. Just before that operation, he was very nice to talk to, though was concerned about my chest cavity problem, which I had had since birth. I received an appointment from him for a check-up about this problem as in time to come this could impact my health.

So Mum once again arranged transport for us with the local volunteer group and we went to see him in June of that year, 1985. He was a rather pleasant man and greeted us warmly. He asked to examine my chest, in particular my pectus concave, which was the name given to my problem. He asked me if I had had any breathing problems or pain radiating from my spine into my chest. I told him that I did sometimes, especially if I walked at a fast pace. He suggested that he could help me with this, though it would involve having a huge, major operation, where my sternum would be broken and brought forward away from the pressure of my spine, thereby helping my breathing, then he would place 2 metal rods to secure it under my breast bone. He told me that it would be a very long operation, about 3 – 4 hours, after which I would be in the intensive care unit for 3 days, then transferred to the ward for another 2 – 3 weeks, depending on my progress.

Well as you can imagine, this was a lot for me to think about, also to take in. He stated that in the meantime, he could put me on the waiting list, though class it as urgent, and he did advise me to go home, talk it through with my mum and have a think about it, as it was a huge decision for me to make, and let him know my answer. There were a lot of things for me to consider as it would involve me having another trip to theatre and more time spent in hospital. On the other hand, if I did have the operation, it would benefit me later on in my life.

The next few weeks I had a lot to think about and consider, all the pros and cons of having this operation. Mum tried her best to advise me, but at the end of the day, it was my decision as I knew that it would fall back on Mum to look after me once again. After two weeks, I came to the conclusion that this operation had many benefits for me, especially as I got older, so I rang the hospital to let them know that I would like to go ahead with the operation and asked if they could send me an appointment. As my surgeon had classed my operation as urgent, around 8 weeks later, I received the news that it would be performed on the 12th of September, 1985. I was not to eat any breakfast on the day, just drink plain water or tea.

19

My Last Procedure

Me and my mum arrived at the hospital early in the morning. I felt quite apprehensive, anxious, nervous and worried, hoping that this one would be a success for me, as all the others on my spine had not been. I did not want to go through such a major operation with the same outcome, just like the others; I really was placing all my hope and confidence in my cardiothoracic surgeon. I was shown to the ward, a mixed ward and I was asked to have a shower, the usual checks were made by the nurses, temperature, blood pressure, weight, height etc.

Then my surgeon came to see me along with the anaesthetist, he told me that my surgery would be later that day in the afternoon and he reassured me that everything would be alright. Mum stayed with me all that day though not on the ward. They came for me around 4.30 pm that same day and I was taken to the theatre. I do remember that I did not feel too well at all when I came around; I really did not believe that I would survive such a massive operation. Apparently whilst I was under, I had been babbling on about what I wanted to do with my life, I could not remember this at all. When I did eventually wake up, I was placed on a breathing machine in the intensive care unit. I do remember my surgeon coming in and saying that my operation had gone well, he was pleased and that I would be in the intensive care unit for 2-3 days. I reached out my hand for Mum, she was there for me like she had always been throughout my life. She had a very concerned, worried look on her face, I believe that it was the breathing machine. Looking back, it must have been very frightening for her to see me like that.

I progressed very well and 2 days later, I was transferred to a single ward on my own, which was good for me, my own room. As I had drains in either side of my body, I had to be careful not to move about quickly as I could pull on them. Around 9 days later, a nurse came to check the 2 drains, she removed them from me and placed a dressing on them both. She told me that in 3-4 days I would be having my stitches out and depending on my progress, I would be allowed to go home. This was really great news, so I rang Mum at home to tell her. She was as pleased as I was. Once the drains came out, I began to feel so very fatigued and tired all the time, I just wanted to sleep, sleep, sleep. A nurse then came to remove my stitches, there were only 4, the other ones being dissolvable. She told me that the wound looked good and clean. My surgeon came to see me later that day, he stated that he was very pleased with my progress and that I could go home the very next day. I was very happy about this as the hospital bed was very uncomfortable and lumpy.

Mum came up to see me that night, she was really surprised that I would be coming home. It was 2 weeks in all, not a very pleasant experience for either of us at the time, but since then it has proved to be very beneficial for me and it is one operation that I'm glad I had, though, like the Harrington rods in my spine, the 2 rods under my breastbone would have to be removed too in time, as they would come through my skin, just like the rods had; it seemed that my body rejected any metal in it.

I arrived home at the end of September, back to my own bed and surroundings. It felt strange at first, lying on my bed, however, I did manage to catch up on all the missed sleep I had had whilst in hospital. Sleep and rest were what I needed. I now had to recuperate and get stronger in myself, ready to face any of life's challenges, which were around the corner.

There was a huge challenge which came to me the following year in the August/September time, the year now being 1986. We had a nice spring, warm pleasant, summer, autumn was just around the corner. Mum having been placed in care whilst a young child, had developed bunions which recently had begun to trouble her. She was in a lot of pain with them most days. After having been to see the local chiropodist, she was advised to have them removed as this would alleviate all her pain. A few weeks later, Mum decided to get some advice from an orthopaedic surgeon, who like her chiropodist agreed that an operation on them would solve all of her problems and that she would be able to get back to walking and dancing again which, unlike me, she loved. I guess this is what kept her slim.

So, Mum received a hospital appointment for September 1986, nearly a year after my chest operation. Initially, of course, Mum was concerned and worried as to how I would cope with her aftercare when she arrived home again. It was arranged that social services would have a carer to call each week who would collect our benefits, do some food shopping, and washing and hoovering up which was needed on a weekly basis. So began this different role play for us both, in that Mum had always been the caregiver to me, looking after my every need since the day I was born and now it was my turn, with the help of a carer. So began a tough challenge for me, was I up to it I asked myself? Or would I fail? Then the day arrived for Mum to be admitted into hospital for major foot surgery. Just how would I cope? This felt rather daunting to me, a tough challenge no doubt.

20

Roles Reversed

Mum was in hospital for 2 weeks, I visited her every day, it was really very hard for me to leave at the end of the day as I stayed with Mum for around 6 – 8 hours each time. It felt strange for me to go back home with no one there as I had never lived alone before. It was very hard for me to see her in so much pain, following her major operation, though I was with her every step of the way and before I knew it, it was time for Mum to leave the hospital to come home. So I arranged for her bed to be brought down from upstairs into the lounge; my bed was already in the lounge, which was good as I would be there if she wanted anything in the night.

I was really pleased for Mum to come back home and we both settled down to a daily routine with Mum having to go to the hospital every morning for 8 weeks to have physiotherapy. Following her major operation, this really took its toll on her, whether it helped her I am not sure, up to that point I had never cooked a meal in my life, Mum having done all the cooking; though it was a challenge for me, I really tried my best.

3 months later, Mum received an appointment to see her surgeon for a check-up. Well as usual I went with her and he was very pleased with her progress but from experience, most surgeons say this anyway. However, Mum was still in a lot of pain; she could not walk far and in my opinion, she was worse off now than before the operation. The following 2 years and onwards were a real struggle for Mum as her operation had been negligent, as was her surgeon, but after Mum consulted various solicitors for some form of compensation, nothing came of it. This was most upsetting and disappointing for her as the operation had left her in despair with a very painful pair of feet which would only worsen with age. During this time, I cared for

Mum, and her feet too, and in the weeks that followed I would dress them for her.

The year was now 1987, Mum had been writing to a nice gentleman who lived in Lincolnshire. In time they met up and he was very kind at first, but like most of Mum's gentlemen friends, he became very clingy and needy, so much so that as she said to me on a few occasions, she felt that she had another child on her hands.

At this point in our lives, we made a decision to move, mainly due to personal family problems and complications which involved Simon my brother, who was now trying to find out where we were living, following the breakup of our whole family which he caused. Neither me nor Mum wanted anything to do with Simon as he was a nasty, vindictive bully whom we did not want in our lives. During the family break up, after the death of my lovely brother, Darren, Tony the youngest brother and Mandy my sister decided to all stay together, as Mandy was in touch with her own dad at that time, after having married early, aged just 18 to a soldier in the army. So, that just left me and Mum together with each other.

The time arrived for us to move home. Mum's gentleman friend was invited to visit her in our new home. Sadly, things did not work out for them and in 1989 their friendship ended, with Mum being hurt once again. That year, Mum suggested that we go away on holiday abroad to Greece as she felt that we needed a break away. So we flew to Greece for a 10-day holiday. We had a nice relaxing time, though the very hot weather was a bit too much for us both at times.

After our holiday abroad, we were glad to be home again and back to our usual daily routine. 1990 was now on the horizon and with it, there were more problems for Mum with her feet and she had constant neck pain, so for us, it was a round of doctor's visits, along with chiropodist appointments for her. Throughout it all, I was there supporting her. My operations and hospital visits had ended, it seemed to me that things had reversed and now it was Mum's turn to be cared for.

21

More Changes To Come

At that time, me and Mum were living in a 3-bedroomed house with stairs. We were both struggling to climb them most days. It would often leave me breathless, and with Mum's feet and back in more pain, something really needed to be done about this situation. A 3-bedroomed house with stairs was not really ideal for either of us. Mum approached our local council and she was put on the local council housing list for suitable accommodation such as a bungalow or a ground-floor flat; this referral was classed as urgent due to our individual circumstances and health needs.

Around 14 months or so later, in the spring of 1991, Mum received a letter from the council, regarding a suitable home for us. There were some 2 bedroomed bungalows being built that year and we were on the list to go to view them once they had been built, so for us, this was great news, things were looking up for us both at last. Later that year, around August time, we went to view the bungalow which was to become my home for the next 21 years. We were so excited to move into this bungalow as both our health had deteriorated, living in a large house, with stairs and a garden which neither of us could look after, so we paid a gardener to care for it for us.

After living in the bungalow for 2 weeks, we found ourselves with some new next-door neighbours who invited us both in for a chat and to get to know us better. Well, Mum was very hesitant at first, as she did like to smoke at that time, whereas these new neighbours did not. This was brought up in our conversation with them and Mum being Mum, really took offence at this, hence the fact that after that, she never went into their house again. This caused a rift between them and us and at that time none of their family members would acknowledge or even talk to us, so it really was not a good start to being neighbourly. For most of that year of 1991, we were busy with jobs like putting up nets, curtains, pictures and the like, really putting our stamp on the place, which was good.

In time, we would get to know some of the other neighbours in the area, however, Mum would always seem to hold back for some reason. As I was rather a shy person, I always found it hard to make friends; I was introverted, whereas Mum was always the extroverted one. She was a very sociable person back then and could talk to anyone and everyone. For some unknown reason, 9 years later, this all changed as Mum changed completely. From the kind, caring, loving, sweet, happy-go-lucky Mum who really enjoyed a good laugh, who had a great sense of humour, and a good personality, to someone else whom I did not recognise. This felt as if it had happened overnight and now I was living with a completely different person, it seemed like she had had a personality change.

Christmas and New Year came and went; we were still buying things for our new home. Around March time, we both began thinking about having a break away somewhere, though not in England, so we both settled for going to Majorca in June which we did. I really enjoyed flying, we left a very cold, rainy England and arrived in sunny Majorca for 10 days of sunshine, sand, sea and rest. Whilst in Majorca, we took in a lot of trips around Majorca and in doing so, we got to know the island well. The Spanish people were really nice and friendly, we were taken for sisters, by the locals, which made Mum feel quite good at that time. We had very dark brown hair, all-natural, with Mum having olive skin so of course we were taken for being Spanish; our ancestors did come from Spain, many generations before, so this was no surprise to us.

Most nights of our holiday in Majorca were spent being chased around by either the Spanish waiters in our hotel or Spanish taxi men, sometimes just the Spanish men in the street, or even a club we visited, it did become quite tiresome for us. However, before we knew it, it was time for us to say goodbye to

Majorca and return home to England. We really enjoyed our holiday though, and we would return to Majorca a few years later.

Upon arriving home, we unpacked our cases and settled down to our routine, which we both had gotten used to by then. We would go into town once a week to have a look around the shops, get some grocery shopping done, and then stop for a pot of tea and a cream cake or snack at a local café, after which we would always get a taxi back home as we both had spinal problems, we could not carry too much shopping in one go. My scoliosis continued to bother me more it seemed the older I became, also Mum suffered a lot of pain every day in her spine and feet; since having her foot operation, her mobility gradually reduced.

The year 2000 was a turning point for both of us, though I was still the same kind, caring, thoughtful person, Mum completely changed in every way. She used to have this saying, "One day the worm will turn." I never knew what it meant, not until the year 2,000 when the mother I loved, cherished and thought the world of, even putting her on a pedestal, just changed before my eyes; she became bitter, sad, selfish, critical, sarcastic, complaining about most things. She would put me down, any chance she got, which was every day. I could not do anything right, I could not please her in any way and she did not appreciate anything I did for her; in her eyes, it was not up to her standard. She would constantly compare me with herself and everyone around us, such as our neighbours. She became very, very negative in every way. The only thing at that time that seemed to please her and make her happy was her faith which was mine too.

We had previously studied the Bible with the Jehovah's Witnesses having had quite a few Bible studies over the years. Like Mum, my faith meant a lot to me. Looking back now, it was my faith that stopped me from making the biggest mistake of my life and I'm so very glad now that it did as everyone has a right to lead a happy, peaceful life.

22

Changes Once Again

Mum suggested around May time in the year 2000 that we both should have another Bible study with the Jehovah's Witnesses, so as I always did to please Mum, I agreed and a few weeks later we were assigned two male elders from the main Kingdom Hall to call every week to study the Bible with us, with the aid of Bible-based publications to enable us to fully understand just what we were learning.

However, at that time, Mum smoked cigarettes. She would have one before they arrived, this habit bothered her a lot but in due time, mainly because of her health problems, she would eventually give them up. Because of Mum's progressive health concerns, I was given more responsibility in that I would go to the local post office weekly to get both our benefits, collect Mum's medication and then do a little shopping. At that time, we had a care firm every 2 weeks to go and do the big shop for us, which was very helpful.

So, I guess in a way I became Mum's main carer, and our roles now had changed. Mum did not like or appreciate it at all, she rebelled against our new roles and she disliked change in any form. As I had not been out to meet people and mix, sadly, I had no friends in the area. Mum too had not made any female friends since moving home, though this did not bother her as she preferred it that way for us, with just her and me.

In time, she came to expect and require so much from me, that living with her at that time, I felt that I was in a pressure cooker. I was just not allowed to be me, she took over everything, every aspect of my life and I felt completely overshadowed by this dominant, forthright woman in every way possible. I began to feel that my true identity was being extinguished!

We had our lovely weekly Bible study now to look forward to and over the next 2-3 years, it became the highlight of my week, as there was nothing else in the week, just sadness and despair, so depression began to overwhelm me on a daily basis. In time, I became quite angry and irritated in myself, so much so that I went to see my doctor about all these conflicting feelings I was having regularly. He told me that I was clinically depressed and prescribed me some anti-depressant tablets which would help me. I have been on them for around 18 years. They did seem to help me at that time, though I did have to address my anger problems, so in time, at Mum's prompting, I went to see an anger management counsellor on a weekly basis. She would talk to me and encourage me to tell her exactly how I felt and the reason for this. She would listen to me, it felt good for me to tell someone who understood this problem I had. So, for around 3 months in 2005, I went to see this counsellor, my depression then did not seem so bad.

During this year, I began to lose weight. When I went to see my doctor about this, he told me that he felt that I had irritable bowel syndrome as I was stressed most of the time, with the bad situation at home. This did not help, so he prescribed me some medication to help ease the symptoms, which were pretty bad at the time. My food did not seem to be doing much for me as up to that point, I had always had a good appetite. I really loved my food, now it felt that it was a real effort for me to eat. I did not enjoy my food, in fact, looking back then, I did not enjoy anything in life, apart from my faith. I would often talk to God, hoping that He heard me. I felt that he understood this awful situation I found myself in. I was so sad and depressed in myself every day, that in time to come, it got so bad for me that it was even an effort getting up in the morning. I felt that there really was nothing or no one to look forward to seeing that day.

At that particular time and in the years 2004 to 2005, both my and Mum's finances became a big problem for us as we had a joint account. For some reason, the tax office contacted me, as well as the Income Support section of the Department of Health and Social Security. A few days later, I received a letter from the

Fraud Squad at the same place as the Department of Health and Social Security who had been informed that fraud had been committed by me, also the bank had written to me, to say the same thing. So, this meant I was being investigated by the fraud team at our local DHSS office, as both me and Mum had some savings in our joint account which apparently took us over the amount we were allowed to have. We were both on benefits at the time, I was not however allowed to have any savings, something I was not aware of at the time. After this, Mum had a home visit in 2005 from the Pension Credit people, they came to interview her and to take a written statement from her, which they did.

The Fraud section at the local Department of Health and Security contacted me too, in the July of that year. In the meantime, both me and Mum moved our money into another bank account in a different town. They wanted to see me, with all our bank account statements and details of any other savings I might have had at that time. By this time, Mum had been informed by the Pension Credit people that she was allowed to have her savings, as it would not affect her other benefits, so she was off the hook as it were.

Me, on the other hand, well mine was a different story entirely, they wanted to interview me as this was a very serious offence, one which could entail a prison sentence for me. As stated previously, I did not realise that I could not have any savings, as we were no longer able to go abroad on holiday, due mainly to Mum's progressive health problems, the money in our joint account just mounted up, as we were unable to spend it on anything.

The day finally arrived for me to be interviewed, a taped interview by the fraud officer at the local DHSS office in town. This day came, one which I had been dreading, so as I was going there on my own, I was very nervous, anxious and quite stressed. All I could do was to tell the truth, whilst at the back of my mind, all I could think about was could this be my last day of freedom? I did not know what would be the outcome for me, I just prayed that it would be a positive one.

23

The fraud officer asked me all these questions about how the amount had built up over the years, and why we had not spent the money. I did explain that neither me nor Mum could now go away on holiday, mainly due to Mum's progressive ill health, so it just mounted up, though at the time I had looked into having a walk-in shower fitted in the bungalow which would benefit us both as neither I nor Mum could get into the bath safely, due to our spinal problems. He made a note of this. I explained to him that none of this was done purposefully to defraud the DHSS, I genuinely was not aware that having savings would affect my income support benefit. As it was my idea in the first place to have a joint account with Mum, I felt that the blame for this was all down to me, so I took full responsibility. However, in the meantime, we had moved our money into another bank for safekeeping. He wanted to know the whereabouts of the account, something which I never disclosed, as Mum had told me not to involve her in this, but to keep her out of it, so this is what I did, I was loyal to my mum.

After around 45 minutes, the interview finished and the recording tape was turned off. The officer told me that in 4 weeks, I would receive a letter with their decision as I had co-operated with him, he did not feel that there would be a court case, though it would mean that I would have to pay back the overpayment of income support. Every two weeks the money would be deducted from my benefits, right until it was all refunded back to the Department of Social Security. So, it was a relief for me to know that I would not be going to court or prison, which Mum seemed to think I would be, or perhaps she hoped I would be.

Once I got outside, I breathed a huge sigh of relief, said a little prayer of thanks and rang Mum to let her know that I was on my way home. I was so pleased to get home that day, Mum did not seem very happy though, as she really believed that I would be going to prison! She could not understand,

"How you got away with it!" she said to me, these were her own words to me on returning home that day. I told her that I informed them I was unaware that I could not have any savings whilst claiming income support allowance. She seemed quite annoyed and agitated by this outcome, then she even accused me of paying the fraud officer off to keep quiet about our savings, I told her that was not true.

I did receive a letter 5 weeks later from the DSS to state that I would have to pay back all of the income support benefit overpayment, and the rate would be set at £44 per month. At that time Mum read the letter and shouted at me saying once again, "I do not know how you got away with it!"

It seemed to me at that time that she was a little disappointed that I was not going to spend some time at Her Majesty's pleasure but I can assure you that I was very pleased they believed me.

Autumn that year was nice, not too hot, not too cold, just right, though our relationship had become a little strained. Mum's health persisted to be a downward spiral, Christmas came and went so quickly that year, as did the new year, so before we knew it, 2006 was here with a whole lot of other problems for us to cope with.

Mum began to complain more and more about her spine and foot pain, she had severe arthritis in both. She was advised by her doctor to rest up more in the daytime. Her doctor increased the pain relief she was on and gave her morphine to take to help with the pain. The morphine was a very strong dose indeed, so much so that she now spent a lot of time in her bedroom, asleep if not resting, so I did not get to see much of her at all during the day. This did not really bother me as at least she was not patronising me, putting me down constantly, being nasty or critical with me, or directed at the neighbours or the carer who would call every week now to do the big shop for us. So, at least I was still needed to go to our local post office, to collect our benefits, collect any medication or pay any bills which needed to be paid. This I did on a weekly basis, Mum even found fault with this. Mum found fault with most things back then, everything I did was not right with her, there was just no way of pleasing her, no matter how hard I tried, and I did try so much that towards the end of our relationship, I had no interest in doing anything for her, whether it be dressing her feet, filling hot water bottles for her back pain, making her endless cups of tea, going to the bank for her, taking care of all her correspondence. All these things I did for her, I would really feel proud to do because I truly loved and respected her and to me, she was my hero, someone to look up to. I put my mum on a pedestal, she was my world and nothing was too much for me. Well, she just killed all this, it was like our mother/daughter relationship had fractured and was at an end, dead in the water so to speak.

Mum always made me feel so low about myself, there was never any affection or kindness now like there was before. She changed during this period, my depression really reared its ugly head and my anger began to be a problem, so once again I went to see the doctor for some advice. He recommended that I should see an anger management counsellor who would be able to help me cope with these feelings. He put me on the waiting list and 5 months later I received an appointment to see a lady anger management counsellor.

This appointment was in August of 2006, at that time I began to suffer badly from irritable bowel syndrome which was mainly brought on by all the stress and anxiety that I was having to cope with on a daily basis at home. Once again, my doctor gave me some medication for this, which did help up to a point, though Mum seemed to think that because I had lost so much weight, around one stone during the past 10 months, I was now about seven stone, that I was somehow "going to the health shop to buy weight loss pills". In other words, I was losing weight deliberately to get some attention from my doctor or people in general, this was Mum's theory anyway. This was how Mum's mind was working at the time, after this I found her in my bedroom looking in my wardrobe to see if I had hidden them in there!

I started to visit the anger management counsellor every week, though as you can imagine, I was always on edge with her, as I knew that Mum would be checking up on me by ringing my mobile phone to see where I was and when I would be coming back home. I felt that the counsellor picked up on this, though I did enjoy our sessions, it did help me to talk to someone who understood just what I was going through at that time. However, she did feel that if the situation at home were to change, then it would be much better for me. I got the impression that what she was really advising me to do was to get out, move out, and for me and Mum to go our separate ways. We were no good for each other, as we were together 24 hours a day, 7 days a week. I was at home most of the time, so I never got a break from all the stress and anxiety, only when I went into town or the post office. I had no social life, no friends, no neighbours to talk to and confide in, there was just no escape for me, sometimes I felt like a prisoner in my own home.

At that point in my life, I had no escape plan, I was trapped like an animal. I had no confidence in myself and no self-esteem to even think or contemplate doing something about my situation. Though a few weeks later after this time, I would come to actually consider the possibility that it could be done and that I would be able to change my life for the better.

24

Someone To Talk To

My birthday came and went that year, 2006. I was 45 years old then, still living with my mum, still in this same boring town. I decided in the year 2007 that I would go to a night class to do a cooking course which would benefit both of us, especially Mum as she often said that I had no idea how to cook. Her being a complete vegan at that time did not help matters, though I must admit I was not very adept at cooking, truth be told I did not really enjoy it. This new year it would change as I would really try my hardest to make some decent vegan meals for Mum.

Myself, I was a vegetarian at that time, though I did enjoy some vegan food. We had a lot of soya products, tofu, rice dishes and vegetables were aplenty in our home. However, once again, whatever meal was put in front of Mum, she would find fault with it. Most days now I did not enjoy eating any of the meals, so this made no difference to me anyway. I was just too sad and depressed to eat anything, I really did not feel like any food. I felt that my vegetarian diet was doing me no good, there was just no substance to it, most days I felt weak, tired, lethargic and generally poorly in myself. I told Mum that I would be going to a cookery class in January of 2007, she just laughed at me and shook her head, with no encouragement from her at all.

The Christmas that year was so cold, as was the new year. We had some snow, though I was so glad when the time came for me to go to the cookery class, perhaps I could learn something and it was positive too. As it was on an evening, I would make sure that Mum was resting and she would have everything, her cold water, her hot water bottle and that she was comfortable. The class was for 6 weeks and during that time, I learned a few things and I got to make a meal that night to take home with me which was good. January came, as did February and before I knew it, it was the month of March and Easter would soon be here, as would Mum's 74th birthday, which she did not make much of, neither did I now.

I used to make a lot of Mum's birthdays, though no matter what I bought for her, there was no pleasing her. She was so miserable in herself, it seemed now that she did not even like flowers in the home, which was unusual for her as she always loved her flowers. So, because of this, I did not buy much, just a card, that was all I felt like giving her.

The summer of that year was quite hot, we would have an electric fan in most rooms. At that time we had a mobile hairdresser, who would call to cut and style both our hairs. Mum would delight in calling me to her, so when it was my turn she would not say much to me, though I was aware of what was going on and the atmosphere in the home or as Mum would say, "my home", was terrible. Most visitors would notice it; however, visitors were very scarce at that time.

The Autumn was really nice. I had lost more weight, so the weakness was there most days. The mobile hairdresser had decided she could no longer call as she did not like the awful atmosphere, so I contacted another mobile hairdresser, she was a young lady who would call on a regular basis, every 3-4 weeks. She would have to use the back door; Mum's orders, of course, as she did not want to be disturbed whilst resting. Mum even managed to insult her in time and that would mean only one thing, once again we were without a mobile hairdresser. In October of that year, it was just before my 46th birthday, another lady came to take care of our hair. "Let's hope she stays longer than the previous ones," is what I thought to myself. Thankfully she did, which was good.

My birthday was a quiet time, I did not want any fuss, especially from Mum. As we did not drink and I had a cold that evening, we watched some television together but even this pleasure would be knocked on the head eventually in time, just like me. I was not even allowed to use my laptop in my bedroom as it was too noisy for Mum, who was next door in her bedroom.

I cannot remember much of the winter, Christmas even of that year. We still had a carer who did the weekly shop for us. 2008 was on the horizon, but for me, there was nothing to look forward to, every day was the same for me. I yearned to have a friend, just someone I could talk to and confide in, as Mum just wanted me all to herself, to become a recluse like her and in time, when you live with someone like that, you get to be like them, think and feel like them. In time, I became very critical of people in general, neighbours, especially our neighbours whom I would see when going to the local post office and shops.

I began to think negatively all of the time, about everyone and everything in general, to me this became normal.

Well, the new year of 2008 was here at last; "Let's hope it's a better one!" I thought, and happily, for me, it was. This year I decided to go to another cookery class in June, after having tried a nighttime cookery class, which did not go down too well with Mum. I tried a jewellery-making class at the start of the year, it was okay, though some of the equipment we used was quite hard for me to operate. I did not talk to any of the people in the class, as I did not know how, I guess I had become introverted, due to the situation at home. The cookery class was interesting, we made a lot of vegetarian meals, no vegan meals as the vegetarian ones could be modified. After we made the meals, we all got to take them home with us. However once again, Mum did not comment on the meals I made. There really was no way of pleasing her. I tried, I did, so in the end, I made the decision not to go again, I did miss the company though.

Mum's health problems became a lot worse in the year and she began spending more and more time in bed resting and every other week the doctor would visit for one thing or another.

In August of this year, my youngest brother, Tony, sadly passed away from a fatal heart attack. Apparently, Mum had been ringing him at home regularly, his son would answer the phone and when Tony came to the phone, Mum would put the phone down. This had been going on for a little while, Mum knew that Tony had passed away and she did not think to tell me this news.

It made me so sad and I did think that it was very cruel of her to keep it from me.

It was only 4 years later after I had moved away from Mum, that I managed to find all this information online about my brother. It was a shock to me. It was most upsetting and distressing for me to find this out, I just could not believe that my mother, or any mother in fact, would keep this from her daughter as I had a right to know!

The autumn was not far off now, September was here, not long to go before my 47th birthday. It turned out to be a quiet one for me, this is how I liked it. Mum at that time had to go to see the doctor and specialists about her spine; like me, she had scoliosis and osteoporosis. I would escort her to the hospital in a taxi, or perhaps to the doctor, sometimes she would make a sarcastic remark to me. As I had become used to this, I just ignored it, that's the way she was. Looking back now, I guess that in a way I felt sorry for her.

Sometimes in the week, I would go on the bus to our local shops, if we ran out of milk or something. Once again, Mum would be non-stop ringing me to see where I was. I would turn my mobile phone off, as I knew that it would be her.

Our neighbour next door had a daughter called Carol, who worked in one of the shops, one day we got talking and she commented that I looked very sad. Well at that time, I really felt I had to talk to someone, I needed to, it was to unburden myself, so I explained to Carol just exactly what had been going on and how Mum had been treating me. Well, Carol was very surprised to hear this, as she often visited her dad, she would come past our house, she just did not realise what had been happening, as her family had not really had anything to do with us after Mum had insulted her Mum when we first moved in. She told me that if I ever wanted to talk to someone, her dad was always there, also she could be there too, depending on the day and time. She told me that I would be most welcome, which was lovely to hear. Well, I guess one prayer had been answered.

25

At the beginning of December that year, I was feeling very low, down and depressed mainly due to the situation at home. I felt that I needed some company and someone to talk to, so I decided to go next door to see either Brian, Carol's dad or Carol herself. Brian answered the door, invited me in, made me a cup of tea and we had a chat. He listened when I told him what had been going on. Once again, he had not realised the very fragile relationship both me and Mum had at that time. He felt for me though, I could tell this. He told me that I was welcome to call and see him anytime I was feeling depressed, sad and low, he would be there.

In time, Brian became a good friend, my confidante, a form of escape for me. In a way, Mum came to resent this fact, as I did tell her where I was going at the time, she knew that I was only next door, not far away. Brian himself was elderly, being 89 years old at that time, she would often refer to him as my daddy, "Are you going to see your daddy today?" she would say, quite mockingly. Whilst I was there, she would constantly ring my mobile phone, this was just to annoy and wind me up.

Apart from Brian and Carol, his daughter, I had managed to make a friend of Kathy, one of the ladies who worked in the local pharmacy near where we lived. I am still in touch with her, having known her now for around 30 years. Brian and Carol had a big family, a few of them knew me and Mum from when we first moved in. Around one week before Christmas, I was rather low in myself, so I decided to go and see Brian for a chat. Well, Carol answered the door and once again I was made most welcome, with Carol running around making tea for everyone there.

As Carol, Brian and all their family knew that I did not celebrate Christmas, they did not get me a card or a present. I was glad about this. Once again, before I knew it, the New Year of 2009 was upon us. Like all the previous years since the year

2000, once more I did not relish this year, I just had to make the most of it, I guess by being able to do a little shopping, collecting both our benefits, going to the local post office and, of course, going into town once a fortnight though once again Mum would be constantly ringing me on the phone to see when I would be home. This I could never understand as when I did get home, there was no conversation from her, no she just wanted to dominate and control me, also to make sure that I was there at her beck and call all the time. Sometimes I felt like a slave to her, not her daughter. However, a few weeks later, I got an invitation from Carol to have lunch with her and her brother Mike, which I did. I really enjoyed this, the company too. I was able to go as Mum was having a visitor that day, so I was required to make myself scarce, I did not mind as it made a nice change for me.

Mum's life at that time would revolve around various doctors calling most weeks to help with her pain control. The carer would call to do our weekly big shop, at first Mum would allow me to go with them, in time though this was stopped as she said that the carer took a longer time going with me than on her own. So I did not even have this free time away from the very tense, fraught, difficult situation at home.

Then one day Mum suggested that she would like the Jehovah's Witnesses to visit us and for us all to go through some of their magazine articles with them. As we had had 3 or 4 Bible studies in the past, Mum felt that having another one would be pointless as we were both well versed in Bible knowledge, more so Mum of course as Mum had at least 45 years of knowledge of their faith and believing in it, whereas me, I was brought up with it from the age of 17 years old.

We all had a Bible study as a family when Mum married her second husband, Jerry, who at that time seemed very interested in her faith, also my sister Mandy. However, I do feel that the only thing Mandy was interested in at the time was the teenage lads in the area, going by our front lounge window.

So once again, I agreed with Mum, mainly to keep the peace, whatever peace there was at the time. Looking back, I was not as keen as Mum to start another study of the Bible due to the tense, awful atmosphere in our home. I felt that she was being hypocritical, but that was how Mum was. However, around 2-3 weeks later, two male congregation elders knocked on the front door which I answered and they came into the lounge to be greeted by Mum smiling and happy. We then started a nice study of the latest Watchtower magazine. As we did so, I wondered just exactly what was Mum up to and where was she going with this. She only did things for a reason, usually to benefit herself.

26

Nice Company At Last

So once again, we started a nice study of the latest Watchtower magazine; we were both asked questions, which Mum of course would always answer first. When the two elders left our home, after being offered refreshments by me, I would often feel that it was hypocritical of Mum, and if I could have gotten out of this, I would have done so, though I did know that it would be me who would suffer the consequences so I kept quiet as to how I felt about our weekly study. It did not stop me from feeling guilty about it though!

However, I must admit that as neither of us had many visitors at that time, I did look forward to seeing Steve and Pete and in time they became our friends, which was nice. These visits would last most of the year, we would commemorate the "Jesus" memorial at home together, like we had done for the past 20 years or so, with Mum taking the lead as usual. My mum was such a forthright, dominant person, very, very strong mentally, not so bodily as she would never give up or give in to the intense pain which racked her body every day. She would carry on whatever. I guess in a way I'm the same, I never give in to the pain which sometimes controls my thoughts and feelings, though, unlike Mum, at this time I do choose to go without any pain relief due to all the adverse side effects. I much prefer natural medicine, like acupuncture which I have found does help my spinal pain along with heat therapy and massage.

So around November time, Steve and Pete asked us if we would like to continue with the various magazine studies in 2010. Well, I was not too keen to, but before I could reply, Mum said, "Yes, that would be great and perhaps in the meantime me and Lydia will take the time to read the whole of the Bible." This we indeed did. Looking back, I was so glad that we did; however, it would take up to 14 months to complete, perhaps more.

2010 was now here and at least we would both look forward to seeing Steve and Pete, though in time both of them would be too busy in the ministry work and we would be studying the Watchtower and Awake magazines with 2 lady witnesses, one of which I did not favour, mainly due to stirring things, making nasty comments and insults. These comments became very hurtful to me, which was really another way of Mum putting me down once more. She could not say anything nice or positive about me at all, at times this became very tiring for me.

That year we still had the carer doing our big shop, also a lady to do the hoovering up, once a month, along with a window cleaner who would clean the inside and outside windows. I was still needed though, to put the net curtains up at the windows or curtains even though I was not allowed to use the washing machine or microwave oven, which I had bought because our gas oven was now too low for me to get down to. Mum would insist that I not use the microwave oven, so it would be at least another 2 years before I got to use it myself in my own home.

This year Mum would lay down another rule too, that we could not watch any television at all, this was in the summer of 2010. Well, I was a little upset about this as I enjoyed watching the tennis at Wimbledon, so I had to resort to listening to it on my portable radio in my bedroom, with my headphones on, so I did not disturb Mum who was resting next door. The summer that year was nice and hot and I managed to see my newfound friends, Brian and Carol who would listen to me, trying to understand just what was going on in my life next door and why Mum was treating me like this.

My birthday that year was okay I guess, I did manage to have my hair styled in town, it looked nice and sleek at that time, though when I put my wig on top of it, it spoiled the effect. Both of us had been wearing wigs at that time for around 10 years, this was Mum's idea, I never liked wearing them, they would itch and become sweaty, especially in the summertime. Sometimes I just felt like pulling it off my head, it really did get on my nerves! As I said, it was Mum's idea to wear these wigs as having our hair coloured regularly was becoming too much for Mum and me with our spinal problems.

Although, in reality, it was too much for Mum in time, I began to resent wearing these false things on my head. Mum sensed that I did not like them, she would poke fun at my grey hair underneath my wig. At that time the neighbours in the area began to suspect that we were both wearing wigs. Some days I would think that the taxi men and people in the local shops knew about them too, especially in the hot weather we had that year.

27
New Rules

So, now, I was not allowed to watch any television, nor could I have broadband for my laptop. Though I used a dongle, Mum still found fault with it and complained that it was too loud for her, as she was resting next door as I used it in my bedroom. I really loved listening to the radio, as I loved music so much. Mum did not want the radio or my CD player on, she much preferred the calm, the quietness. I, on the other hand, thought that it was eerie and strange, as Mum like me really loved the radio, but not now. So, sometimes when I went to the local shops, I bought Mum some flowers which she used to love years ago, though now it seems that even flowers were not allowed in the home.

The hot, pleasant summer gave way to a mild autumn time that year things in our house stayed the same. We were getting through reading the Bible, and the 2 witness ladies called to see us every week. Mum would often praise the younger one to me and compare my faith and knowledge to hers, during the study. I did not get much of a chance to answer, as either Mum or Amy would rush to reply, so in the end I began to keep quiet and pretended that I did not know the answer.

One day Mum suggested to me that I should make an effort to go to one of their study groups in our area, so to please her I did. Though I did not feel confident doing this at that time, as I had not mixed with people for such a long time, I found it most difficult as I could not say no to Mum. I went but sometimes I did not feel like going due to the strained, tense atmosphere at home.

I only had Brian and Carol to talk to about the situation, I was constantly depressed and low and my sleep pattern was odd too. My doctor had put me on anti-depressant tablets for my depression, although he did suggest that I go to the local hospital to be assessed by a psychiatrist nurse, this was voluntary on my part, he felt that this could help me in some way. So, one day in the September of 2010, I went to see her. I travelled by taxi to the clinic; this was to assess my levels of depression. After around 10 minutes of waiting, she called me in and we talked, discussing the situation at home. I told her how I felt about it all. She asked me if I had lost weight as stress can do this. I told her, yes I had as I did not enjoy my food or anything at all really.

She decided to weigh me, I was six stones 4 lbs which was nothing, so no wonder I felt so weak, tired and ill most of the time. I had no energy, no motivation, no life really, I was just existing on a day-to-day basis. She listened to me and advised me that the best thing for me to do was to move out of the home, away from Mum, as she was the cause of all my problems, stress, sadness, depression, anxiety, heart palpitations and high blood pressure, more than it should be. It was no good for me to live there under such distressing conditions she said. Well, I was quite amazed at this, as I did so much for Mum, I was her main carer and she needed me at that time. I had never thought about moving away from her. This thought really did scare me, having lived with Mum at that time for 48 years, being dependent on her since my birth, over the years we had done so much together, gone on holidays, laughed and cried together, she had been my best friend, someone I could turn to and depend on, she had always been there for me. I just could not imagine my life without her in it and here this nurse was advising me to branch out, go it alone, go find a life for myself, somewhere on my own.

When I returned home that day, I told my mum. She made a sarcastic remark to me, and I told her that everything went okay, she really believed that they would have taken me in and admitted me to have psychiatric treatment, to basically throw away the key. I did come to believe that my mum had written a letter to my doctor, asking him to get me to see a psychiatrist or possibly treatment. She was rather surprised that this was the end of the matter and that I would not be having any more follow-up appointments.

In the following months of that year, I had a lot of things to think about and consider though my birthday that year was another quiet one, like the last, just the two of us. The winter was cold again, as was the start of January, a new year was now here, 2011, this was when I would make one of the best decisions of my entire life.

28

The start of 2011 was when I made plans for my escape as it were. By this time my weight had plummeted to 5 stones 11 lbs. I had weighed myself on our scales, something I had not done for around 3 years. As I looked down at the scales, I just could not believe it, mind you I did not enjoy my food, nor life in general, nothing really. Years before the change in Mum, I had a great appetite, I loved my food and would often finish Mum's food off for her. However, now my life had no pleasure in it, I was not allowed to listen to the radio, watch TV, listen to my music CDs or use my laptop, so what did I have? I have always loved music, Mum knew this so in a way this was a form of cruelty on the part of Mum to stop it. She seemed to wallow in my misery every day.

January that year seemed to fly by, I was glad of this, as I never liked the month. February was quite okay, though cold with a northerly wind. March came, but to me, it seemed the same as February, as one month was much the same as any other. However, by then, I had made up my mind to get away from Mum and the constant tirade of daily abuse, by moving away. I started looking on my laptop in the day for council flats or even a nice park home to rent or buy, though not in this town. I still had all my savings after all, so perhaps I could manage to either buy a park home or if not, part rent/part buy, this is what I thought I would do. I purchased a park home magazine and started to look for park homes. There were quite a few and I could move anywhere in England. After looking through the magazine, most of them were down south, out of my price range.

I decided to visit my local council housing offices and explained my situation to them. They told me that I would be only offered a one-bedroom flat in any part of the city and that there was a 3 - 4 years waiting list for the council flats. As I did not want to stay there and live in the same town as Mum, they could not help me so it would not be worth me going to the council's own waiting list for a property. It would be up to me to find somewhere to live as I wanted to make a clean break away from Mum, away from the town, the area, the doctors, the neighbours, everybody really, any memory that connected me to the place, a place that I had lived in for 20 years, somewhere I had come to dislike greatly.

I decided in the April time of that year to write a few letters to the managers of a few park home sites around the country. There was one in Norfolk, one in Leicestershire, one in Lincolnshire and one in Lancashire, so I then sat back and waited for them to contact me, either by letter or by mobile phone as I had enclosed this with the letter.

April that year, around Easter time, was a very pleasant one, the Jehovah's Witness ladies were still visiting us for our study and in a way I began to look forward to seeing them, as other than our weekly carer, and hairdressers, we had no visitors. Mum at that time had contacted a care firm, who would call and take her out and about in a fold-up, push wheelchair. I do not know where she went, as by now we were living separate lives; she did her thing, and I did mine. When we did meet up, there was never much talking in between, our relationship had become like a stalemate. I would sometimes hear Mum on the phone in her bedroom around 11 at night, speaking to someone, my name being mentioned, of course, I guess she was calling me to someone though I often thought who could it be at that time of night?

One night, I decided to find out just who it was, as we had a phone in the lounge and at about the same time, she was speaking once again on the phone, I crept into the lounge from my bedroom, picked up the receiver and listened in. There was no one on the other end of the phone, it was just Mum talking to herself. How very strange, I thought, this must be for my benefit, it was just one of her cruel controlling ways, she really loved to see me suffer.

This is what I had to put up with, Mum knew me too well, she knew that I would listen in, she really played me, very cunning, very clever I thought at the time, well she will not take it well when she knows of my plans. At last, my favourite 2 months of the year were here, May and June. I just loved May as all the flowers, plants and shrubs were settled in bloom, the days were longer and the nights were lighter too. However, when Mum was well enough, we would go away on holiday together, abroad and in England.

I am so glad that I managed to visit various countries and, of course, to fly as I just love going on an aeroplane. I never imagined at that time that I would ever travel on a plane on my own abroad, as I did not have the confidence, something else Mum took away from me. So, I had to make the most of the situation I found myself in, though some days it was a struggle for me and very monotonous too.

Mum's carer would call for her every week to take her out, this would give me time to use my computer to check out various park homes in different areas and to contact them. Most in the south of England were too expensive for me, so I decided to look elsewhere in the Midlands, Derbyshire, Leicestershire and parts of Lincolnshire. I did contact a few, but they had none to sell at that time. I did visit a couple, not too far from Stamford in Lincolnshire, but they seemed too far away from any amenities such as shops, post office, the main town, as I did not have any transport, they were not suitable. I continued to write to a few more park home sites after this, but I had no replies from any of them. This left me feeling a little despondent, though I would not give up, I just knew that there was one nice park home waiting for me.

This writing and ringing the owners of the park home sites went on from April right up to the end of August, during that time my life living with Mum in the awful, awkward atmosphere in the home became unbearable for me, so to escape it, I would often visit Brian next door, just to talk. Sometimes Carol would visit him while I was there which was nice, they could both see the effect of the mental and psychological abuse on me, as now I was under six stones. Also, I made a friend of a nice lady who worked in a nearby chemist. She had often said that my mum was very controlling on the phone when ringing about her medication, so she could empathise with me. We would often have a chat about my situation. I'm still in touch with Kathy to this day, it is good to talk to her as she understands exactly what I went through. At that time, there were not many people I could turn to, the witness ladies would not believe that someone as poorly as my mum would be treating me like she did; to them, as to most people, she was a lovely, kind, gentle, sweet lady, this was just an act on her part, one she acted very well and convincingly too.

The summer was nice, though quite hot that year. Mum did not like the heat. June came it was not too hot, July was a little too hot and humid, though it brought the Wimbledon tennis which me and Mum used to watch on television, though not this year, her rules again, so I decided to listen to it on my radio with my headphones plugged in.

Apart from going out with her carers, Mum just lived like a recluse, this is what I feel she wanted me to become. I did not want this kind of life, I needed to talk to people and see people. Even so, sometimes it was hard for me, as I did not have many topics to talk about, my life at that time was really just on hold, at a standstill if you like, however, this was not to be for much longer.

29

Good News On The Horizon

One day, I went to see Brian, Carol was there, she said that her sister and brother were going for lunch and would I like to go with them? I said no at first, but then I thought no, I will go, it would have to be the day that Mum went out with her carers, I would let her know the day, which I did the following week. I was really looking forward to this to do something normal for a change.

Carol waited for me outside her dad's house and we all went out for lunch at a new restaurant. Carol treated me to lunch. We had a good laugh and a good time was had by all. Just as we were leaving the restaurant, Mum started ringing me to check where I was. So as not to spoil a nice, pleasant day, I ignored the phone, this was the type of thing she always did to me and I came to get used to it.

When I was younger, me and Mum would go on our holidays abroad, she was so different back then, she was someone I could look up to, we were friends and in those days, we would go everywhere together, we were really very close. Looking back now, she is the Mum that I will always remember. We would have a laugh, share a joke, we liked the same music, clothes, television programmes, interests, hobbies and so on. I would say that she was more like my sister than my mum. As my real sister, Mandy was completely the opposite of me, we never really got on, she was not like my mum in her nature, although she did inherit Mum's attractive good looks, eyes, her physical attributes, but not her personality; as Mandy was selfish, vain, self-absorbed, more confident than me, brazen, thought a lot of herself. She loved the boys, men too, and all the attention she received from them.

I guess that she was just wild at heart, not respectful at all of her own body, you could say coarse also in her speech. All these things she did not inherit from Mum or me. Like my dad and brother Darren, she just loved to have a drink, going to most pubs on a night out, she was really like my dad totally. She was different from her own dad, as he did not like to drink much, he was a kind, homely, respectable family man as I said earlier, Mandy was on her own.

Before I knew it that year, August was here, we were on the brink of Autumn. I was upset as I had not heard anything from the park home site owners in the Midlands, whom I had contacted earlier in the year. However, around the end of August, a lady visited us at home. Mum answered and invited her in, she wanted to see me as she explained that she had received my letter and that she owned two park home sites in and around the Leicestershire area, though the one site which I would have preferred, she did not have any park homes for sale. However, there was a park home on the other site and she asked if I would be interested in it.

At once I said, "Yes, when could I visit to look at the park home?"

She stated that she could collect me one day the following week to take me to view it. So, I gave her my mobile phone number so we could make definite arrangements. After she left, I just could not believe it, at last I thought I could escape this dreadful, melancholy, awful situation here, this was my dream come true, there really was a way out for me at long last, and to me, it had been such a long wait.

My prayers it seemed had been answered at last!

30 - More Problems To Come

That same day and all the days that followed I was very excited, positive and looking forward to seeing the park home; my very first home, my own home. The next week could not come quickly enough for me, at last, that day was here. She arrived at the arranged time, then we were on our way. Before we viewed the home, we stopped off to have a drink and some lunch, which was nice. I had to turn my phone off though, as up to that point, I had had 6 missed calls from Mum, she just did not leave me alone on days like these, she turned up the pressure.

We arrived at the 2-bedroomed park home in a nice area of the main town, around an 8-minute walk into the town itself and just a 2-3 minute walk to the nearest shop and bus stop. Well, I just loved the park home, it was fully furnished, and some of the furniture I did not want, but that was okay. It had a big kitchen, cosy lounge, hall, a nice sized bathroom, a small second bedroom and a cosy, bigger bedroom which would be mine. It was pointed out to me that she lived right opposite to me in the bungalow. Being a very trusting person at the time, I did not realise that I would be dealing with gypsies, as the site was owned and managed by a family of gypsies, headed by her, Lizzy. As it turned out, she ruled everyone in her family, even her husband, she was the worst of the lot.

Lizzy wanted an answer that day, as to if I would be buying the home, so I did not have any time to think about it at all. I just knew this was the only way for me to escape, to get out from all the stress, hurt, anger and sadness brought on by Mum and her hurtful, controlling ways, so I told Lizzy yes, I would be buying the home, would she require a deposit to secure the sale?

To which she replied that she would like half the sale price and the rest upon the completion of the sale. She presented me with a certificate of deed sale, she told me as I had never bought a property before, this was all new to me. She stated that this sale was done just between the two of us and that we did not need to involve solicitors as this would cost more, to which I agreed at the time, a decision in time I came to regret bitterly. So, everything was arranged between us. I told her that I would need at least 2 months to get everything organised as I had to buy another sofa, arrange a removal company and help for me with the packing. I did not have a lot of furniture, there were things in the home I had gone half with and I would have to buy a fridge freezer, as in the park home there was not one. We were looking at the end of October, however, what I did not know then was it would not be until the following January 2012, before I could move in, as Lizzie's husband had to go into hospital, a London hospital and she wanted to be with him. His operation was in November, his recovery time was given 8-10 weeks, then we were looking at the beginning of January 2012.

This meant that I would have to put up with the abuse a little bit longer than I expected, although I do believe that Mum felt that I would change my mind about moving and leaving her, so in the following months she really laid the guilty cards on me, telling me most days she did not know how I could leave her when she needed me. Well by that time, the truth was I did not need my mum or all the hurt and abuse she made me suffer at that time, I was confident enough to know my own mind, just exactly what I was capable of. I employed a care firm to help me with the move and they took me shopping for items for my new home, though once again they would not come inside our house due to the dreadful, tense atmosphere which Mum would cause whilst they were there, so they would knock and wait outside for me. It was good for me to have some company at last, I really enjoyed our little trips out.

I would go to visit Brian every week to let him and Carol know my progress. The 4 months seemed to drag by to me. October came and with it my 50th birthday. I decided to visit Brian. Carol answered the door, I told her that it was my 50th birthday, so Brian gave me some money, which was very kind of him as being a pensioner, he did not have much. I thanked him and told him I would buy something nice and useful, which I did.

Carol made me a cup of tea and we had a good chat, along with a catch-up on the news, then after about an hour, Mum started to ring me once again, and it was promptly turned off. I started to shake inside and get stressed, my anxiety started up and I began to tremble, I always did when she started her controlling, bad ways, as I had these feelings every day of my life at that time, they would sometimes make me feel completely ill.

I said my goodbyes to Brian and Carol and returned home to Mum who once again was very sarcastic to me, especially when I told her that Brian gave me some money for my birthday. She shouted at me, saying that was disgusting and I should give it back to him, I should not be taking money from a pensioner. Once again, she made me feel so ashamed and small, just like a scolded, scared little girl. Anyway, this time I ignored her and said it was a very nice gesture, they both made me feel very welcome.

The next few weeks after that were tense as we did not speak much, well that was fine by me. Lizzy would often ring me with progress of her husband. November that year was miserable, not too cold, just wet and windy, I would still go out with my carers each week, by this time, I had nearly bought everything and written to all the people I needed to.

Then Christmas time was on us, we never did celebrate it because of our religion, but it did not bother us, though Carol had said would I like to call around 3-4 days before Christmas? She knew about our faith, so she never gave us a card or present, which was alright. So, 3 days before Christmas, I went to see them both. Carol answered once more. What I did not know was that quite a lot of their family members would be there, however, I was made welcome. Carol was running around making everyone a cuppa, cake, sandwiches, pies etc, being a very good host like she always was. We all had a good chat and a laugh too, it was great for me to be able to mix with people of different ages. Then it was time for me to leave. When I got back, Mum did not say much to me which was good, something I had gotten used to by that time, at least that way no hurtful words or arguments were started.

Christmas that year we had no snow, I was really looking forward to the new year as it was going to be my year. That year, I was going to be released from my prison bonds, awful life and captor. Well, that's exactly how it seemed to me. Now it was time for me to celebrate, January 18th 2012 was not too far ahead, I waited, marking the 18 days off in my diary.

However, the next day Mum decided to talk to me. She asked me what date I would be moving and if could she have my forwarding address for the council she said. I told her that the date was the 18th of January, to which she replied that she wanted me to move out on Monday 6th January 2012 and not any later. I said that I would clear it with Lizzy first as earlier was fine by me, though I did give her my new address which turned out to be a big mistake for me.

The new year was a very quiet one for us, it always was in the area we lived in, as I was the youngest one living there and most of our neighbours were over 65 years old.

The first of January 2012 was here, at last, a new life, a new home, a new year beckoned me. I wondered what it would bring. I was very scared about the move, I really loved my mum, she meant the world to me, though no one should treat you like she did me, I did not deserve it. I will always love my mum, though I knew this time there was just no going back, it was time for me to move on.

31

Free At Last

There were only 5 days to go before I moved out, I was excited, though apprehensive too, as living with someone for 50 years and then all of a sudden leaving home, going it alone, it was just a little scary for me to contemplate. I knew I had to do this, to be free, to be myself and have a life, as living with Mum, I felt that I had become like her in many ways. I was introverted, sad, negative, depressed, no confidence at all, no sense of humour, just bland and boring.

New Year's Day came and went, though the next day I did see Carol at the local shops. I told her that I would be moving in 4 days' time and she said for me to call her and her dad, Brian before I left that day, this is exactly what I did.

I rang Lizzy on the 3rd of January to tell her that the removal van should be with her around 3 p.m. on the 6th of January. I asked her if she would not mind buying me some flowers, I thought that this would be a nice touch. The next 2 days flew by and then at last the 6th of January was here. I got up earlier than usual, it was a cold, damp day, we had had some rain earlier in the morning, I had my breakfast on my own that day as Mum was resting.

She got up around 12 noon, upon which she came out with, "I never had any feelings for you anyway." This really hurt me, it went deep. The previous week she had told me, "I will not be leaving you anything in my will," to which I replied, "I don't want your money, Mum." She would often come out with these nasty, hurtful remarks, it was only the week before that she had got all our photo albums out and told me that she wanted me to tear them all up with her, which we did, however, I managed to keep a few of the nice ones. It was as if she was saying to me, "I am going to erase you from life like you are doing to me."

The removal van came around one o'clock. I told them what needed to be taken, as I nipped next door to see Carol and Brian, to say all our goodbyes, though she would be visiting me in my new home, also keeping in touch with me over the phone. So at about two o'clock, it was time for me to go. I felt a rush of adrenalin, excitement, I think. I left Mum in the kitchen and hurried to the waiting van which was to take me to freedom and of course a new life.

A brand new life now awaited me, in a small Leicestershire market town. However, little did I know then that I would be jumping from the fire into a larger frying pan, full of trouble, hurt, stress, anxiety, loss, heartache and much more. I was just so pleased to be released, as it were, I never, ever anticipated what would happen next. Being the beginning of January, it was cold, we had had a covering of snow, I arrived at my new park home around 3 p.m., to be greeted by a smiling Lizzy, who immediately pointed out to me that she had bought the flowers. She led me to my new home and said that if I needed any help to just ask the maintenance man, who was called Pete.

Pete came straight across to ask me if there was anything I needed doing. I told him, yes, there were a few things I could not do, so he set to and helped me. I could not help noticing just how cold it was in the home. I mentioned it to him, he showed me to the boiler cupboard, he had a look at it and said that the thermostat needed adjusting, which he did for me. In the kitchen, there was a microwave already. As I had brought one with me, which I had not been allowed to use whilst living with Mum, I felt that I would not need 2, so I asked Pete if he would like to buy the one already here from me. He said yes, we agreed on a price of £10. However, he never paid me for this, he just took it that day, and cleared off, leaving me to feel rather disappointed in him!

The very next day, I awoke to someone shouting outside, this was to be a regular occurrence at the site. As I went to use my toilet, I found it to be thoroughly blocked, unable to be used, just what I needed on my second day here I thought!

I went to find Pete who came to unblock it, as I would need to use it in due course. I went next door to my neighbour and a nice friendly couple answered the door. I explained to them about my predicament, they made me welcome with tea and biscuits, then Lizzie's right-hand woman came to see me, to say that the job would take at least 3-4 hours before it would be useable. I stayed at my neighbours' house for around 2 hours and upon my return, Pete was still there and the water company had been called for advice. I busied myself with a few jobs, unpacking whilst I waited. Around 2 hours later, Pete knocked to say that it had been fixed and would I like to give it a flush. Which I did, yes it was now okay to use, I thanked him and he left.

By this time, it was around 5 o'clock and as it was January, it began to get a little chilly, so I went to the boiler cupboard. I turned it on and after about 30 minutes, the temperature was the same, so I tried to adjust the thermostat on all of the radiators, it did not make any difference, I still did not have any heat, perhaps there was a problem with the boiler? I decided to go and see Lizzy about it. She said that it had been working, she could not understand why it was not working and sent Pete over once again to check it. He did confirm that there was a problem with the boiler, he would tell Lizzy who would get an engineer to mend it for me.

Around 7 o'clock, an engineer came to have a look at what the problem was with the boiler. He managed to fix it quite promptly, which was fine by me. What a first day this was for me, as by this time I was tired and stressed out. In the weeks that followed, I became more used to the area, making friends with a few of my neighbours which was nice, they even took me to the supermarket for me to do some shopping. Whilst there, Mum began once again to ring me, she kept ringing me, so I turned my phone off, telling her that I was doing my shopping. A few weeks later, Mum started writing her letters to me, some of which I never read, they just went straight in the bin!

The first six months went quite smoothly at the park home site. I got to know most of my neighbours, Lizzie's family, her 2 sons, also her husband who all seemed very illiterate. Looking back, I guess that the whole family was.

In my park home, there was a very low bath which I could not use, so I applied to the local council for a disabled facilities grant and 2 weeks later, an occupational therapist paid me a visit. She was very nice and understanding. She felt that I would be accepted for a grant in which case the council would be doing the work for me to convert the bathroom into a wet room, with a walk-in shower, it would take them around 4-5 days to complete. Around 3 months later, I received a letter from the council to say that the work had been approved and the men would start in one week's time. I was quite excited about having my own wet room which would enable me to have a shower and before I knew it, the workmen were knocking on my door, they told me the work would take one week to complete, which was fine by me. That day, they concentrated on the floor of the bathroom, the next day the bath was taken out, and left outside my park home ready to be disposed of.

Joan, my next-door neighbour came to see me that day as she often did, just for a chat and a cup of tea. We would often take it in turns, as sometimes I would go to her house and then she would come to mine. As the plumber was on his lunch break at that time, she came in and told me that Lizzy had been complaining about his work van being on her nice, precious patio driveway. She did not like that! I said to Joan, "Where else can he park it?" to which she replied, "Take no notice of her, she always manages to find something or someone here to moan about. You will find out what she and all of her family are like to know."

She left about one hour later, the plumber had returned by that time, he told me that Lizzy had confronted him to ask how long this work would take, also how long would his van be on her drive. He told her he did not know as it all depended on the parts being in stock, everything was going to plan as it should. He said that she made him feel very intimidated with her brusque attitude. I apologised to him for her rudeness and he carried on with his work, leaving around 5 p.m. like the day before.

The next day, Lizzy came to quiz me about the work being done. She was quite sharp with me. I explained that the work should be finished by the Monday or the Tuesday of the following week, to which she replied, "Ask them to do it quicker than that, I don't want their van hanging around my driveway." She was very bossy and controlling, I thought, not like the person whom I had bought my park home from, perhaps then she had shown her true colours, but no, there was more to come.

As the days went by, my wet room was looking so lovely, on the very last day, the electrician was to call to check the electrics, sockets, plug points etc. He came in and did a thorough check, which did not take long. He asked me where was the electric metre cupboard located. To which I said I did not have one as I paid Lizzy monthly for the electricity I used. She had one, which was outside my park home. I took him outside to have a look at it. He asked me if she had the key to it. "Yes," I said so he went over to see Lizzy about the key. He came back saying that the electricity came off the one in her house and fed to mine, which was illegal so this would be the reason that I shared a meter with her. He told me this was not right; I should have my own electricity meter cupboard.

Well, I was amazed at this information, I had no idea. He told me that he would have to go back inside her home to find the original source of electricity, which he did, though Lizzy was not very happy about it all, she told him so abruptly. The electrician returned to me saying that the woman was as "Mad as a dog about it!" She was most abusive to him, "shouting and going off on one" he said. Well, what a way to go on I thought.

The very next thing, Lizzy was banging on my front door. She pushed by me and rushed into the kitchen, ranting and raving as she went. She screamed at me, "Get them out of my home, I want them gone!" to which I replied, "It is my home and they are doing a job for me!"

She made me feel so very small in my own home, not to mention how she made the workmen feel, the disgusting way she spoke to me and then swearing and shouting as she left. Honestly, I thought at the time I had never ever seen in my life anything like it. She just reminded me of a very spoilt little girl wanting her own way all the time. Little did I know then that this was just the tip of the iceberg, there was a lot worse to follow in the days ahead.

32

More To Come

I apologised to both workmen for her outburst. The electrician told me that he would not be calling at my home again. He finished his checking of the plugs and sockets quickly, on leaving he was most upset about her awful attitude, this was not to be the last of her outbursts. The plumber came back the next day with his boss who wanted to check over his work. They arrived in the morning and his boss was very pleased, as was I to have my own wet room.

After that episode, Lizzy started to complain to me about my garden, amongst other things. She would often ask me to wash her personal items for her. As I felt obliged to her, I did, though she did make me feel very uncomfortable, as did her husband and 2 sons. All the family gave me the creeps though, especially her husband, he was so strange. In the weeks that followed, I would often see him or one of his sons hanging around my home, this was sometimes on a night too. I realised that all this was to make me feel threatened and vulnerable, which it did, all her family were the same, nasty and horrible, just like Lizzy. I began to think that I would like my very own electricity meter, so I contacted EON to ask if they could call at my home to fit one for me.

I began to anticipate Lizzy's reaction to this, though it was my legal right to have one, as I did not want to keep paying her family for my electricity, as sometimes it went off at night, so it could be very dangerous for me if I got out of bed and fell. I once did this and I hurt my back, falling over a chair in my bedroom. It really shook me up and made me feel even more vulnerable.

Two weeks later, a man came to see me from EON. I showed him Lizzy's meter cupboard and before I knew it, Lizzy and her husband were outside their home, shouting abuse at me and the man from EON, who told me that it was illegal for Lizzy to run my electricity supply to my park home from her own electricity cupboard and that I should have my own. That way, it would not be cutting off at inconvenient times, like on a night time.

He went to have a word with Lizzy and her husband about the electricity supply. She told him to get off her property and clear off, though he ignored this abuse to come back to tell me that I should be hearing from EON in the next 2-3 weeks about fitting me a new meter in the same electric meter cupboard, the only drawback being that he would have to lay another cable or pipe from off her main electricity supply in her home and run it along to mine. This meant that Lizzy would have to give her permission for him to enter her home. I was just so pleased that the job was going to be done, as they did their best to stop it.

The workmen from Eon arrived a few weeks later and once again Lizzy began her abuse of them, shouting and screeching, they took no notice of her rants, they laid the pipe along from her home to my meter, in all it took them around 40 minutes to complete the job. This was the one thing I was very pleased to see being done as it would benefit me, as I knew that she had been overcharging me for the electricity. The council also, lowered the path leading to my park home, once again Lizzy and her husband tried their best to stop the work as it needed to be done for me, however, they both failed.

By this time, I had lived there for just over one year. So, I decided to do some voluntary work in one of the charity shops in the town, which I did, I really enjoyed it. I managed to get my park home looking very smart and nice, I was proud of this. I contacted a care agency so that they would be able to take me to the supermarket to do a big shop on a weekly basis, that way the carer would have to carry the shopping, not me, as I was unable to carry heavy loads due to my spinal problems, this still applies now.

Me and my male carer had just arrived home one day, I was just about to shut the front door when Lizzy lunged at me and tried to force her way into my home. In my haste to try and stop her, she trapped my arm in the door. My carer tried to help me as we both managed to close the door, all I could hear was her shouting abuse at me through the letter box. My carer was very concerned about my arm which was now hurting. He suggested that we report this physical abuse to the police, so he took me to the police station where I told them what had happened and how she had attacked me, just like a mad, rabid dog. After this, I went to my local walk-in health centre to have my arm looked at as having osteoporosis, I have to be careful not to fall and break a bone. The nurse told me that it was alright, nothing broken, though it was bruised, so she advised me just to keep an eye on it and to take paracetamol tablets for the pain, which I did. This attack really frightened me as Lizzy was quite a stocky, strong woman who had a very fiery temper on her.

The police came to see me later on that day. She denied everything of course though they did advise me to stay away from her, to keep my distance, this would be hard for me as I still had to pay her the ground rent, so I decided to give this to Pete the maintenance man. A week went by and I never heard or saw anything of Lizzy, which was good. Then one day, she came to my door to ask me to do some washing for her as her husband was in hospital again and she did not have time to do it. I said sorry, no, I could not as I had enough to do here. She left but I could tell that she did not like what I said.

A few days later, after this, I was planting some bulbs in the front of my park home when Lizzy's husband crept up behind me and threatened me by saying that he wanted me gone, he did not want me living there, he was very nasty, abusive and menacing to me. I came inside very scared, anxious and upset, this was their way of frightening the residents on the site, it was definitely working with me! I rang the local police to tell them about this threat, they advised me to contact victim support, which I did, and also to write down times and places when the verbal abuse happened to keep a diary of every time it happened. That same day, I contacted the local council to inform them of all the abuse that they were subjecting me to on a regular basis.

In the following weeks, I would see Lizzy's husband hanging around my home. He seemed to be watching me and this made me nervous. I was advised to visit my local Citizen's Advice Bureau to see if there was any way that they could help me. When Joan called to see me the next day, I told her what Lizzy and her husband were doing to me, the constant harassment and abuse. They were nothing but bullies, my mum was bad enough and I certainly did not need this. Joan advised me to stay away from Lizzy and all her family as she knew that in the past, they had done the same to the man who had lived in my park home and he had to move out in the end as he was so intimidated, scared and frightened of them both.

At this point, I was too scared and on edge when I went out and more so on my return. It got so bad for me that I really dreaded returning home as I did not know just what or who was waiting for me there.

One evening, there was someone banging on my front door, as it was around 9 o'clock I did not answer it. The next thing they were banging on all the windows, this really frightened me, then I heard a voice shouting abuse at me through my letterbox, it sounded like one of Lizzy's sons so I decided to ring the police. They said that they would be around in 15 minutes, which they were.

I explained to them what had happened and they went to see Lizzy and her son returning to me to say that neither of them knew anything about this and that I must be making it up. In the weeks that followed, they kept up this kind of harassment and bullying. Lizzy began picking on me and it seemed most days her husband was either near the edge of my garden or walking by my home day and night. This particular day, he knocked on my door in the afternoon. I did not answer it to him as the police had told me not to have any form of confrontation with Lizzy, her husband or any of her strange family.

Looking back now, I feel that all of them were so very strange, even the maintenance man, Pete. A few days later, I was on my way out when Lizzy came up to me shouting nastily, "We don't want you here, I want you to move, so get out or you will regret it if you don't!"

I just ignored her comments and carried on walking, she did not like that at all. When I returned home that day, I wrote down all the times the bullying and harassment occurred. One of the final straws came for me, when I came back home one day after working in the charity shop in the town, as I approached my home, I found all my lovely flowers which I had planted a few months before, under my lounge window, ripped up and thrown around about my home, no guesses who had done this. I was most upset and the very next day, I went to visit Joan, I told her about it and she like me, was surprised as to the lengths that Lizzy and her family would go to frighten a resident to want to move away from the area, this is exactly what they wanted me to do.

33

Due to all the harassment and abuse at that time, I was stressed out most days, not sleeping well at all, very depressed, alone and scared as to what was going to happen next. It got to the point that I began to feel so scared, frightened and anxious that when I went out, I did not want to come back to my home. My first home, my own home, which I had made nice for myself and was very proud of. During this time, I decided to buy a budgie for company. She was all white, I called her Melody, she was the first female budgie I had ever had, though she had a character, I guess I spoilt her like most people do with their pets.

After buying Melody, I went to see the Citizen's Advice Bureau at my local council, who listened to me, they told me that I had done the right thing to involve the council, the police and the victim support people, though as I was classed as a vulnerable adult, they felt that I should ask the council for a social worker to call at my home, just to keep a check on me. That same day, I went to see the council about this and they told me that a duty social worker would be in touch with me soon. However, in the meantime, as I felt so frightened to go out and return home, I should ask the local police for some form of protection. This I did, I received a letter to say that they would be visiting me the following week, which was good.

The next day, I was tidying my garden up and Lizzy's husband crept up behind me and said, "I am going to get rid of you. I want you gone from here, do you hear?" He smelt of alcohol and had an awful, nasty look in his eyes, it really terrified me, so I just hurried into my home, quickly shutting the door.

Once again, I rang the police and informed them of this nasty threat, a death threat, as it is what it sounded like to me. For the next 3 days, I did not go out, when I did, I got a taxi into town. On my return home, I thought to myself well if they started abusing me, at least I would have a witness in the taxi man.

The Monday arrived, the main or head police officer in the town came to see me. I told him everything, all of the abuse, harassment and various threats they had made to me, how it was so bad now that I was too scared to go out and return home. He told me that no one should have to live like that, he advised me to move out, sell my home and leave as soon as possible, he was concerned about my safety and well-being. He said that perhaps the council would have a flat or something for me. It was worth asking them, but to do this as soon as I could. The next day saw me at the local council offices, they told me that there was a 1-2 years waiting list for accommodation which did not help me. I left there feeling very disappointed, though not defeated. I decided to buy the local paper to see if there were any private, rented properties suitable for me. I noticed that there were some new one-bedroom apartments being built in a village just five miles from the town, the advert gave a contact number to ring if you would like to arrange a viewing, this I did the very next day.

I spoke to a woman who said that most of the apartments had been built, she had about 4 for me to view, so we arranged a time and day for the end of that week. As I was still having my carers call, I asked if they could take me to the viewing of the apartments, just for a second opinion and some advice.

When I first saw the apartment complex, I was most impressed, it was next to a nursing home, so one of the staff led me and my carer to the woman who looked after the apartments. I was shown 2 on the upper floor and 2 on the ground floor. I knew when I saw the end ground floor apartment that this was the one for me. I left feeling very excited, knowing that I had a lovely, new clean home to move into. The only thing I had to do now was to tell Lizzy that I would be selling my park home and moving out, I thought to myself, "I wonder how she will react to that news!"

Well, guess how she reacted to the news? A few days later, I contacted a local estate agent to view my property to give me a price for it, they did call round, though Lizzy was out that day, her husband watched the estate agent leave. The next thing they rang me to say that Lizzy had been in to see them, once again she had been abusive and nasty to them, telling them that I had a cheek and it was only her and her family who had the right to buy my home from me. They would no longer be interested in my home as she said that Lizzy and her family had a bad reputation in the area for making trouble, being so nasty and issuing threats to people so that was the end of that!

"Oh great, I thought" as I put the phone down, "what do I do now?"

A few days later, I approached another estate agent and they too were interested, though when I told them my address, the man told me as they had had trouble with this family in the past, he advised me to advertise my home privately as I may have more success. All this was very stressful and upsetting for me. I did not know what to do once again, I got advice from the Citizens Advice Bureau who suggested that I have a meeting with Lizzy to see if we could come to some amicable agreement on the sale of my property and how much she was willing to give me for my park home, less the 10% cut for her, which everybody on the site had to pay.

The next day, I plucked up the courage to go and face her, however, no one was home, so I went to see Pete the maintenance man, to ask him to pass on a message to her, when she returned, which was 2 hours later. There was a knock on my front door and Lizzy's husband stood there, I could smell alcohol on him again. He told me that they would give me £12,000 for my home and no more. As my home had been valued at £45,000. I was not going to sell it for less than a third of its value, so I told him that the price was not acceptable to me.

His reply was sharp, "You will never sell it, me, Lizzy and our sons will make sure of it!"

He then left me feeling very distressed and upset indeed.

Joan came to see me the next day, I told her what had gone on, how much they were offering me for my home. She, like me, was disgusted about this, though advised me what other option did I have, if I wanted a quick sale, which I did as I could not cope any longer with all the abuse, threats and harassment. It was now making me feel ill, I was losing weight, not sleeping much, eating little and just worrying about the situation. I told her that I would think hard about it, which I did. The next day I gave a note to pass on to Lizzy and Lizzy only.

She came to see me that night, all smiles, quite happy about me selling up. I told her that I could not wait to move and she stated that I would be getting around £10,000 for my home. She would instruct her solicitor to draw up the much-needed documents of sale and I should be hearing from him. I told her that I would require this in writing from her, and she said, "Not a problem."

That done, I began to ring removal firms, not many could fit me in, though I did find one in the village that I would be moving to, it would be in 4 weeks, my move, that way I would have enough time to pack everything. I rang my social worker, he visited me every day with cardboard boxes for me, which were needed. So, each day I started packing my things up, after living there for just 18 months.

I was very excited about the move, though in the weeks that followed, I received no letter from Lizzy stating she would be buying my home from me, also no word from her solicitor. I went to see her twice a week to remind her to do this for me, but she made excuses saying that she had been too busy to do it! I approached a local solicitor to write to her, as once again it was illegal what she was doing to me. I could see myself not winning this one and losing my home to them, well I was not going to have that, so I decided to get a locksmith to change the locks. He came the next day, he had just about finished when she came rushing up my path, screaming abuse at us both. I quickly shut and locked my front door, checking all the doors and windows as I went, once more I rang the police about her abuse and harassment, and once more they advised me to move as soon as possible.

I could not wait for the following week to come around, Monday, at last, was here, my moving day, a nice, new clean one-bedroomed apartment was now waiting for me, this would be the next new chapter of my life, hopefully a much more peaceful, quiet, kinder one for me, with happy memories waiting to be made.

I travelled in the removal van with the two removal men and my budgie. Upon leaving the park home site, I could not resist looking back at my lovely home and thinking oh! I do hope the next resident here has a better life there than I had.

We carried on and I arrived at my new home about 20 minutes later. I breathed a big sigh of relief, saying a little prayer to myself as I opened the front door to my safe haven.

34

My Safe Haven

My lovely newly built ground floor flat had a beautiful view from my bedroom window which looked onto rolling fields with lots of sheep in them. As it was the countryside, I would often see foxes, hares, rabbits, pheasants and all manner of different birds, from ravens to red kites, robins, and pigeons, they all lived in the beautiful grounds which surrounded the 12 apartments. They were all individual. As mine was at the end, I only had one neighbour other than the flat above me. In time, I would get to know all my neighbours, here and around about. As the village was a good size, there were quite a few people to get to know, and for me, it was like starting once again, though I did not mind as perhaps in time to come, I may make a friend of one of them.

Most of 2013 was spent on my new flat, buying curtains, a new bedding set, a new microwave, kettle etc. This took up a lot of my time, also looking after Melody, my lovely white budgie. Like me, she too would have to get used to our new home. Before I knew it, Christmas had come and gone, by which time I had lived here one year. As I was experiencing a lot of pain in my lower spine, I decided to try acupuncture to see if it would help me. I managed to find a lady who only lived 2 miles away from me which was handy.

I contacted her and she came to see me in October. I had the treatment, it really helped me to cope with the pain. After that initial treatment, I would have it every month with Edwina, who in time would become my best friend. As I had done voluntary work before, I began to work in one of the charity shops in the town once a week for a few hours with the intention of making friends and getting to know people more. I advertised in the village post office for someone to do a weekly shop for me, not expecting much from the advert. A young woman contacted me to say that she lived in the same village and could do my shopping on a weekday. We agreed on a fee, time and day. She arrived at my flat the following Monday, she seemed very nice and friendly so she started to do my weekly shop, in time she would also do some cleaning for me, hoovering up as I was unable to do this for myself.

She was reliable, efficient and chatty. I got to know her and her family which was nice. So, everything was going well for me, I began to settle in and relax as it was very safe here, we have CCTV, a PIN code for the main door, an alarm inside the flat, for help too, all these things I liked, they helped to reassure me. My birthday that year was okay. Edwina came to visit me and we went out for lunch which made a change for me.

That Christmas was nice and quiet, as I do not celebrate it due to my religion. I believe in the Jehovah's Witness faith. It did not really matter. When the new year came around, I just could not believe that I had lived here for two years, they were certainly better, kinder ones for me.

In time, I was introduced to all of Edwina's family. She had four grown-up children and a nice partner. I really felt for the very first time in my life that I belonged, that I was part of a very lovely, sweet family. This is one thing which I never felt with my own family, it seemed that they had an air of indifference about them. There was a lot of jealousy in my family, mainly centred on my mum and her closeness with me, especially when I was going through all my spinal operations. Like other families supporting a sibling and their parents at such a distressing, worrying time, when I needed them to be there for both me and Mum, they were not. So, in a way, I have nothing to thank them for. It was once again all on Mum's shoulders, and she never, ever let me down, she was there for me when I needed her. I guess in some way I was there for her too, when she had to go through a few operations, one being an emergency.

In the third year, I enrolled on a few daytime courses at my local library, one was a painting and art class as I enjoyed drawing and I found it very relaxing. It would get me out, perhaps I might make some more friends. The classes ran for 10 weeks from the spring up to the beginning of June. I decided on a little break away at the end of June. It would be a coach holiday, I was a little bit apprehensive about this, having never been on a coach holiday before. The time just flew by, my holiday was here and I would be going to Wales. I was really excited, having never been to Wales before. It was Llandudno, the hotel was right on the seafront, the area was beautiful, quiet and very relaxing, exactly what I needed. I stayed there for 4 days and managed to get to know a few of the guests in the hotel, also on the coach, which was good.

I arrived home on the fifth day, having a taxi to take me back to my apartment and Melody who was being looked after by a friend, so I would be glad to see her. I really enjoyed my break, I came back from it fully relaxed, calm and happy knowing that one day I would return there.

I thought about doing some voluntary work in one of the many charity shops, the problem was, which one? It would be the British Heart Foundation shop. I was to put labels and sizes on the clothes. I was there for around 2-3 hours and I made friends with a few of the women there. I really liked feeling useful, helping a very good cause. This became regular and I really looked forward to going there. The year went by quickly and it was my birthday again. Edwina suggested that we go out for a meal that year, so we did. She came with her partner so I got to know him too. Then Christmas came around, I just had a quiet time with Melody, though at New Year I went to see one of my neighbours as he was on his own. I took a small bottle of white wine and we had a few drinks to see in the new year of 2015. I wonder what this new year will bring me, I thought as I turned out the light.

35

2015 came around, I was still busy doing jobs in my new flat. I made friends with the lady next door, sadly she had dementia so would sometimes forget that I was coming to see her. I also got to know her carer, he was a very nice man and in time he would become my carer as he would do my weekly shopping and sometimes hoover up. Edwina would often call and ask me if I would like to look after Sky, her beautiful dog, for a few hours whilst she was at work. I enjoyed looking after Sky, he would have a run around the grounds here, and then I would take him into the nursing home so some of the residents there could stroke him. He really liked all the attention he was given.

Then one day I decided to take Sky to meet Kathy, my neighbour. She just loved him, he especially enjoyed the cheese and biscuits she gave him. I am an animal lover, I always have been, they give so much meaning to your life, though throughout my life I have always had budgies. Melody was quite happy enough, she did not talk but she could be very vicious and would often give me a nasty nip on my fingers if I was not fast enough to take them out of her cage.

I settled on doing some voluntary work in the Loros charity shop. I had an initial interview and the following week I started working there. I made friends with a few of the ladies who worked there, it was so good for me to get out of the flat, especially in the summertime. The summer that year was nice, we had a few sunny weeks in June, also July. I managed to book a coach holiday that year, to the Lake District which was beautiful. Once again I made some friends from the coach, one of whom I'm still in touch with now.

More neighbours were to move into the flats that year, some of them were near my age. It is a very popular area here being a medium-sized village in the country. I tried to join the Women's Institute, but in time, I found that it was not for me, so I did not go anymore. I would often go to the village post office to have a chat with the woman who worked there. In time, we would become friends and she would visit me at least 3 times a week. The autumn was quite pleasant that year, I would catch the local bus to have a ride out to one of the neighbouring towns, which made a change for me, something to look forward to in the week.

Then before I knew it, my birthday came around. I did not go out, though my friend Edwina came to see me. I had my acupuncture treatment which really picked me up, it was the only thing that helped me cope with my pain, so this was good. In the winter, just before Christmas, we had a small covering of snow being high up here, I guess that we would always be the first to get any snow. Christmas was a quiet one for me again, as it always was, having never celebrated it since I was 18 years old, due to my religion. It really never bothered me, as most of my friends knew not to send me cards or give me any presents. As for the new year of 2015, well who knew what would happen this year?

The new year was quite cold. January seemed to drag by, though I have never liked this month. We had a couple of neighbours move out on the floor above. I had managed to take some nice photos of the snow and scenery around the lovely grounds, as well as my patio area, as everything looked so fresh and clean when it snowed. I bought myself a mobility scooter in the spring as it would enable me to get around the village and to the post office which was very handy for stamps and for me to get my benefits too. In time, I made friends with Lucy, the woman who did my weekly shopping, she brought her young daughter to meet me which was nice. Like me, she too loved animals. She had a few cats and chickens to look after which her daughter loved and cared for.

Around the end of April, my mobility scooter arrived. I was to have a trial run on it, which I did. It really made a difference to me, it enabled me to get to other parts of the village, the only drawback was that I could not get on the bus, so I kept it to travel around here and in the grounds of the nursing home.

In May, I decided to have a coach holiday to the Lake District area again. It was a 2-day break and we went on a boat on Lake

Windermere, which was very relaxing, followed by a coach journey to a lovely plant nursery on the way back home to the Midlands. I came home feeling very relaxed, calm and happy.

Melody my budgie was looked after by the staff of the nursing home, which was good of them to do this for me. I collected her upon arriving home, she was pleased to see me, I had missed her too. The summer that year was not too hot, I really looked forward to working in the charity shop. I would go on the bus, once a week into the town to have a look around the shops, sometimes stopping to go see Mary, a woman I had made a friend of, who worked in a local card shop. I knew her from when I bought my park home. We would have a chat and catch up on news. I am still in touch with her today. That was the year which I decided to have my flat painted, the kitchen, the lounge and also my bedroom. I disliked the magnolia colour, it was too hospital-like, it was really nice and smart when it was finished.

I thought about looking into some day classes at the main library. I enrolled on a painting course for beginners, starting in September, so this was something for me to look forward to, as I rather liked the idea of drawing and painting and that way I would make new friends. June was a mixture of sunshine and showers that year, though I did manage to go on a few bus trips to nearby towns for half a day as I enjoyed looking at the different shops.

July and August were quite hot months, I am not keen on really hot weather, not like when I was younger. The heat never seemed to bother me then, having visited Greece, Spain and Crete with Mum. We both loved the sun and we would sunbathe for most of the day.

So, when September came around, it was just nice with a soft breeze, not too hot which was good for me. I started the painting class, it was for 2½ hours, and we had 15 minutes for a tea or coffee break. Altogether there were 12 of us, a pleasant group, mostly women though, and some of them were very good at painting and drawing. The teacher taught us different painting techniques and styles. I opted to use the acrylic paint, not the watercolour. One day, a lady brought in a nice picture of a lovely cottage with her. I asked her if I could borrow the picture as I would like to paint it, which I did. In time, I had it framed and it now hangs on my lounge wall, my very first attempt at painting. The class ran for 12 weeks and I thoroughly enjoyed it. Before I knew it, Christmas was now around the corner and with it, worry and anxiety for me.

36

Problems For Melody

Melody my budgie began to feel unwell in herself in November of that year so I managed to find an avian vet, the only thing was they were 25 miles away, so I asked Lucy if she could take me there, which she did. I gave her some money for the petrol as it was a 50-mile round trip. In time, Melody would improve as I tried everything I could to help her. That Christmas time was quite mild, although we did have some snowfall at the end of the month and into the new year of 2016. Well, 2016 was here and this was to become a sad, worrying, stressful time for me, in relation to my lovely pets and also for me as it turned out.

The new year brought some snow, just a slight covering, at the end of February. January was rainy dull and miserable. I busied myself with my sewing hobbies, making a few tapestry kits and also making a new duvet cover set for my bed. Sewing seemed to relax me, as I could sew and watch television at the same time. I decided to teach myself how to crochet on the internet. Melody was still not looking well, she was bringing up her food more often now, so in March I tried to find a vet who dealt with birds as my vet at the time could only offer me medication to help her with the sickness, though they did not explain to me why she was doing this.

I could not find a nearer avian vet practice, so once again in March of that year, I took Melody to the vet, who did see her. It was an hour's journey there, Lucy once again took me, she came in with me to support me. This vet was very knowledgeable about birds in general, though he advised me that Melody should be left there, as she was to have an x-ray. I was apprehensive about this, with her being so small, it could be dangerous for such a tiny bird. Anyway, after talking with Lucy, I agreed that she should be given an x-ray at least, then we would know exactly what we were dealing with, that way perhaps she could be treated.

I came away from the vets feeling very anxious, nervous and stressed, just hoping that she would get through this and that in a couple of days, she would be back home with me again. She stayed at the vets for 2 days. On the third day, I collected her, however, sadly for Melody her diagnosis was not good as she had a fatal, digestive gut problem which would only worsen in time. Unfortunately, the vet could do no more for her, he just gave me some advice as to what may help her in the long run, as this problem was very well-known in caged birds.

So, I came home that day feeling very distressed and sad for Melody, though determined to try all I could to help her as she was most precious to me as all my pets were, after all, they were my family. So, over the next 5-6 months, I concentrated on Melody, reading up as to what would help her. I did not go away that year as I did not want to leave her. March and April that year were cold months, and the Easter time was very wet, so I looked forward to May, perhaps we would have some nice, pleasant days, which we did towards the end of May. I would often push Melody out in her cage, which was on wheels, onto the patio to have some air, where she could tweet and sing to all the birds. I would sit out too, reading or looking at my tablet, to get some much-needed sunshine. I did this most days in June, as it was a very nice temperature, 18-20 degrees with a slight breeze, just how I liked it.

Before I knew it, July had come along, it brought hotter, dry days and of course Wimbledon. I really enjoy watching the tennis, especially the men's tennis, so July was spent watching tennis, having plenty of salads, cold meals such as sandwiches and the like. Come the August time, well it began to hot up, so I had to keep my electric fans on during the day. I thought about getting a second budgie to have him come out to fly around, as Melody had never been out of her cage. I wanted a hand-tame one so I managed to buy one from the same breeder as I got Melody from; he was a small blue male bird and he was called Lubie. He had his own cage next to Melody, she did not seem interested in him at all, though Lubie would jump on my hand and run up and down both my arms, he could not wait to come out of his cage. He was around 8 weeks old when I bought him, I had him for about 7 weeks or so, building up a good relationship with him.

Then one day, I went to take the cover off his cage and sadly for me, I found he had died. I was most upset, bereft, I did not know what to do with myself, I loved him so much. I could not understand why this had happened. I contacted the maintenance man who worked here and we buried him in a little cardboard box within the grounds of the nursing home. We buried him the same day he died, it is a day I will always remember, as afterwards I became so anxious, tense and stressed that I began to have a full panic attack. I had pain going down my left arm and in my chest area.

I was just so upset in myself over his loss. As I felt very unwell at this point, I decided to ring the emergency services. Within 30 minutes, a paramedic was at my door. After a few tests and a tablet placed on my tongue to help the pain, which it did, he advised me to get checked out at the local heart hospital, which I did. He took me there that day, I rang my friend to call to look after my pets for me, which she did. However, what I did not know at that time, as to what I would be like upon returning home from the hospital and how my life would be changed in many aspects, in relation to my walking.

37

More Problems For Me

I was in the heart hospital for 3 days, having various tests and being moved around from bed to bed. This did not help my spinal problems, so I would try to have a walkabout. As I was in a tiny side room on my own, there were not many places for me to walk to. On the third day, the surgeon who had been looking after me came to see me regarding all the results of the tests and his diagnosis was that I had had an anxiety attack and that there was nothing wrong with my heart. I had a strong heart, though he was concerned for me as heart problems run in my family. He did say that diet, lack of exercise, drinking and smoking would not help. This did not apply to me, so I felt very relieved that everything was okay. He told me that I could go home that day, which was great news. I rang my friend Edwina to ask if she could take me home and she said that she could, so about one hour later, I was on my way home with a huge bag full of different medication. I could not wait to see Melody again!

I collected Melody that night and found that I was in agonising pain in my lower spine, which felt weak, this in turn made my walking very unstable. The next day found me holding onto items of my furniture around my flat. I felt unsteady and unbalanced, I did not want to fall as having osteoporosis, it would not be good for me. I decided to ring my doctor's surgery and ask for a home visit. Well at first, they were going to refuse me, so I demanded to see someone, explaining all my spinal problems. I did not like this pain, as by this time it was going down both my legs and was very scary for me.

Anyway, that evening a doctor did call to see me. She examined me and told me that I was experiencing nerve pain, that's why it was so painful for me, she prescribed me Gabapentin tablets, stating that she could only give me a 2-3 month course, as they can be very addictive if taken for longer. The chemist delivered them to me the next day, they left them outside my flat front door on a little side table there. I started them straight away as the pain was so intense.

I managed to feed Melody for the next few days in which time I contacted social services to ask if they could help me in any way. Being a vulnerable adult, perhaps they could provide me with some care for the next 2-3 weeks? I was told that yes, they could help me, it would be care in the home for six weeks. A carer would call to help me every day, to prepare a meal, help with dressing, washing and so on. In the following six weeks, I had to learn how to walk again, though I needed some support. So, the nice maintenance man here brought me a walker to help me, which it did, and I still walk with it even now. It just gives me the support I need, especially on hard ground. I had six weeks of care, then after that as I still needed some help and support, I contacted some private care companies, and they came in to help me for the next 8 weeks, upon which time it was the start of November. I was walking and feeling stronger in myself, by that time, though, being in for so long, I had lost some of my confidence. My first time out, I travelled by taxi, it felt really strange to me, though in the following weeks, I got used to going out once again and in time I would travel by bus. Christmas was on the horizon, we had no snow or ice that year, it was rather cold though.

38

The new year of 2017 beckoned, it would be a quiet one for me again, by this time I felt that I would quite like another baby budgie, so Melody would not be on her own. March or April was the best time to look for another budgie, January was dull and dark and a very long month. I always liked February being a short month, no Valentine's cards for me once again. The little snowdrops were poking their heads through the soil in the second week of March, so I had a look on the internet, though at that time there was none at all, even in my area. I thought it would be best to wait until around June or July that year, this is what I did. I managed to find a budgie breeder in a much larger town, as I decided that I would like a lilac-coloured one, not many of them were around, and I would have to wait until later in the year until one became available.

The summer that year was very muggy, heady and hot. As I had booked a weekend away in May, I would not be away in the summer anyway, this was good, as I do not like it too hot. I cannot cope when it gets to 30 degrees heat, I just wilt and melt. At last, September was here and the weather had become less humid and manageable, I would sit outside and take Melody with me. I could listen to my music or the radio, which was nice. A new neighbour had moved in next door, like me, she too liked music, so that was okay.

Edwina came to give me my acupuncture treatment around the end of September, she brought Sky with her and took a photograph of all three of us, Mellow, Sky and me, so it was great for me to have one of Sky and Mellow together as Mellow loved Sky very much. Mellow was given to me by Edwina my friend. October was quite mild at the beginning of the month, so I had a run out to a few different small towns. I cannot visit big, busy towns as I usually end up having a panic attack, though now I can stop them before they start to cause me trouble. I have learnt how to control them, instead of them controlling me.

My birthday was quiet, I did not go out, but I did get some nice gifts and cards from my friends. I do not drink normally but I did have a small sherry that night and I managed to sleep better too.

The end of the month was wet, cold and windy, as was the start of November. I would sometimes go to visit Sean, my neighbour, who used to live next door and then he moved into the flat which had been converted from the tenant's lounge. It was quite a large flat for one person, though as Sean had numerous health problems, he was glad of the extra space. He would make me a cup of tea, we would have a chat and catch up on things, which was good for us both, as like me, Sean had no contact with his family. He enjoyed the company, as I did, especially in the wintertime time as neither of us got to see many people then.

Out came all my hobbies, knitting, crocheting, sewing, tapestry kits and the like, I enjoyed all of my hobbies, they kept me busy. Towards the end of November, the weather changed and it began to get very cold, with a very bitter, cold northerly wind. I do not like too cold weather, especially if I have to go out in it. It is the ice that I am very scared of, it can be quite dangerous. December became very cold too and we had a few snow showers by the end of the month. After Christmas, it snowed all day one day and on New Year's Eve we had hailstones coming down, very big hailstones in fact. I did manage to stay up that year, to watch the Hogmanay show on television. There were some fireworks too, then 2018 was here, another new year, what would it bring?

Though I would not be on my own, having both Mellow, my rescued bunny and Melody my sweet budgie, they would keep me company. Later on, I would write Mellow's story about how he was saved by my friend and just what he meant to me.

39

January was snowy and cold, we did have some ice on the pavement, and also on the side roads. I did not realise just how bad the paths were and I went out on my mobility scooter to the post office in the village. I was okay going there, though, on the way back, I got stuck in the snow, so I had to go on the road to get back home. Fortunately for me that day, there was not a lot of traffic on the road. I did not go out after that for the next two weeks, not until the snow had gone, which was around the start of February.

Well, February soon passed by that year and I would be starting my voluntary work once again, around the third week of March, so I had this to look forward to. All the little bulbs were coming up once more, like the previous year, so spring would not be far off now. It was a lovely spring that year, April came and with it the rain, as usual, though it was mild, not too cold. I went to my voluntary job every week, I really enjoyed it as it enabled me to get out and meet people as I love to be sociable, to mix with young and old, that way I gained more confidence.

May at last was here, my favourite month, as I had booked a weekend away in January for the May time. I was looking forward to going to Llandudno at the end of May. As it turned out, I ended up going there on a train from Derby train station. As the pick-up for the coach was in the centre of Nottingham, my friend Edwina offered to take me there, which she did, just before the spring bank holiday. We arrived in Nottingham, but she could not find the area of Nottingham where the coach departed from, we went round and round for about 45 minutes, by which time the coach had left and was on its way to Llandudno. The next pick-up area was in Derby at the bus station. As we only had 40 minutes to get there, Edwina tried her best to get us there, though the traffic was very busy that day and we arrived at the bus station missing the coach by 15 minutes, so Edwina suggested that I buy a single train ticket to Llandudno, which I did.

On arriving at the train station which was next door to the bus station, I asked for assistance from the staff at the train station to help me with my luggage, which was good for me. I arrived in Llandudno, Wales and at the hotel 2 hours before the coach, so that was good going, however, due to this, I did not get to know many of the people on the coach. I made the most of my holiday though.

I had a very nice, relaxing time, the weather was good most days and the hotel had some good acts and entertainment on each night, which was an added bonus. Before I knew it, the 3 days had flown by and it was time for me to return home. Melody had missed me, I could tell, I was glad to get back home again and into my own routine. June was around the corner by this time, so I rang the budgie breeder, whom I bought Melody from and he came to my flat the following week with a hand-tame, lilac-coloured, beautiful male budgie whom I called Scooby. Melody was not too bothered by him, as his cage was right next to hers.

Scooby was such a cute little bird, he would jump on my hand, run up and down my arms, sit at the nape of my neck, try to nibble on my hair at the neck and nuzzle into it. So, I decided to take him into my bedroom so he could fly around and not get hurt, as there was nothing in my bedroom to hurt or disturb him. He would land on my bed and make his way up my arm, to get to the nape of my neck where he would nestle and go to sleep, I suppose this is what baby budgies do with their mother.

Scooby was very young, around 9 weeks old. I had Scooby for about 4 weeks. Sadly at the end of July, I found him at the bottom of his cage. He, like Lubey, had passed away, he had no symptoms at all of being ill, though I do believe that he was way too young to leave his mummy. Perhaps he was even younger than 9 weeks old. Once again, I was upset and distraught, my anxiety came back quite badly as did my stress levels, and then of course my depression followed.

I had a bad time all of August, September and even October. I tried not to go out and consequently mix with people, when it is bad, I get quite introverted, I just want to be on my own, not see anyone. I did not want the company of anybody, my friends even, though most of them understood this. My birthday this year was not much to talk about, then November came around again, with all the radio and media talking about how many days it was to Christmas.

November began mild, I did not go to my voluntary job after October so I managed to keep myself busy by doing all my hobbies, sewing, tapestry and knitting too. I always feel that the wintertime is worse for people like me who suffer from depression, stress and anxiety, the long dark nights do not help either. December came along with the long, cold days but no snow this year. Then Christmas was upon us once again, then the new year sales, adverts full of holidays, getaways on the television, I just hoped that this year of 2019 would be a pleasant one for me, with nothing unexpected happening.

40

A New Year Ahead

The new year was here again. We had a lot of rain, and cold, damp days but no snow or ice, so I was pleased about that. I did not go out much, as my friend came to do the shopping for me, only this time it was not Lucy as she had told me just before the new year that she was unable to help any more as a new job beckoned her, and she would not have the time to fit my shopping and cleaning in.

In the meantime, I got to know one of the ladies who worked in the shop inside the local post office in the village, Karen was her name. She told me that she goes to Tesco 3 times a week and she could easily do my shopping for me, as she usually goes on a Tuesday. This suited me, so the first Tuesday she came to my flat to collect my shopping list. In time, I came to make a good friend of Karen, as she would do my shopping and stop for a cup of tea and a chat which was nice for me. I really looked forward to seeing her as it became a regular routine for us. I enjoyed her company, though in time this would end as most things do in life.

February came with some cold and wet days and before I knew it, March was here, with all the little spring bulbs coming through. It was quite a mild March that year, the birds were all singing, looking after their young ones. Then there were the little lambs running around in the fields and of course, a family of wild rabbits could be seen very early in the morning, the baby rabbits were so cute! We had the spring sales in the shops which were busy, I did not go to these though, as I usually looked at them online.

Easter time came, the weather being a little cool, we had a small covering of snow at the start of April but it soon disappeared. May was not far off now when I would start my voluntary work again. I liked travelling on the bus, meeting new people, whatever age, and in doing so, helping out a very worthy cause. In June of that year, my friend Edwina told me that her dog, Sky, had not been as active as he usually was, he had been tired, not wanting his food, not like him at all. She had taken him to see a vet who said that Sky had arthritis in various parts of his body, he was in pain and this was the reason for his lethargy and low mood. He was given some treatment for this, which really helped him, though as he was 14 years of age, like us our bodies break down too.

June was a nice month, I managed to go on my early break to Llandudno in Wales for 3 days. When I returned, I noticed that Melody was struggling with her food and regurgitating it back up, regularly throughout the day. So I decided to contact the avian vet and he said to bring her in to be checked over. I asked Karen if she would be able to take me there and she said okay. So, we went to see the vet which was around a 50-mile round trip. Melody got to see the vet, but sadly for me, the news was not good, I was told that there was not much that could be done for Melody, her problem was fatal. So, I set about making her as comfortable as I could. In the weeks that followed, I tried everything I could think of to help her, knowing that time was short.

July came and went, then we were in August, my brave Melody was hanging in there, she like me was a little fighter, she really fought to the end. I believe it was for me as she knew just how much she meant to me. At that time, I said that I would never have another budgie. But as I could not see myself without a budgie or a pet in my life, I decided to have some more budgies.

Most of the August Melody I noticed was becoming weaker in herself. She would sometimes fall off her perch. I would help her back up, and also place her on her swing which she loved. Some days were better than others for her. I decided not to have any more breaks away that year, as I wanted to be here with my Melody. September arrived with some dry, warm days and I would sometimes sit outside to get some nice fresh air.

That evening, I was very concerned about Melody as she had not eaten anything most of the day. So, I put some seed on my hand for her to eat. She did manage a little bit, and then I held her in my hand, I brought her out of her cage and placed her on my chest, gently stroking her feathers and talking soothingly to her. For the following 2 hours, she lay there and in time she passed away peacefully. She was with her mummy at the end. I of course was heartbroken. Melody, to me, was a very special budgie, she meant the world to me, she was my family after all.

In time, I placed her tiny body in a lined box, which I put in my bedroom on my dresser. Before I put her in the box, I gave her a kiss and said a prayer for her. I immediately rang Karen and Edwina, my friends. I was so upset about losing her, they listened to me whilst I cried. I was so glad that at the end of her life, she was with me and not on her own. In the days that followed, I decided to have my Melody cremated. One of my neighbours at that time offered to take me to the crematorium, which he did. As I had to collect Melody the next week, he said that he would take me again, which was very kind of him to do this for me.

I managed to buy a heart-shaped cremation dish for Melody online for her ashes. This sits in my glass cabinet in the lounge, along with a few lovely photographs of her. I will never forget her. Melody was 7½ years old, quite a good age for a budgie, loved very much by me.

As I was so upset over losing Melody, my thoughts over the following few months did not go to other budgies as I missed her so much.

41
My Mellow

However, another sad blow was to come my way with my lovely Mellow, as during November, he became listless and a little wobbly on his back legs. I would bring him out of his cage to let him get some exercise in my bedroom. It seemed that he did not want to run around much, so I offered him his favourite treats which most times he would eat. He much preferred to be stroked by me, I thought at the time that this was because he was getting older, as I really never knew how old Mellow was, as he was abandoned, thrown out on the streets of Devon. So, of course, he could have been 3 or 4 years old when I first took him from my friend Edwina, who had rescued him.

Mellow as a very, very special rabbit, like my Melody he meant the world to me. I had both Melody and Mellow painted by a local artist, their portrait is hanging on my lounge wall, I often look at it and remember all the happiness, love and joy they both brought into my life.

A few days later, I came to clean Mellow's cage and found him collapsed on the cage floor, he was unable to stand or get up on his own. Well as you can imagine, I began to panic, so I rang his vet's practice, who advised me to bring him in straight away. So, I rang Rachel who worked in the upstairs office next to the nursing home. Rachel would often help me clean Mellow up as she had rabbits herself, she really understood them and I knew that she would help me. She said that she would take me and Mellow to the vets, I knew in my mind that Mellow was seriously ill, I had to stop myself from shaking, being anxious and worried.

We arrived at the vets, Mellow was examined by the vet and returned to me with his diagnosis. Sadly, he had had a massive stroke and there was nothing that the vet could do for him. So, I had to make one of the hardest and most upsetting decisions of my life, this was to have my sweet, mild, loving Mellow put to sleep so he would not suffer any more. So, I gently kissed his head, looked into his beautiful eyes and told him that I loved him and I would never ever forget him, after all, he was family and I had had him with me for 4½ years. Well as you can imagine, that day I was inconsolable as I had lost two of my beautiful, cherished pets.

I felt my depression gradually creep back over the following weeks of losing my Mellow, I became very low and down in myself. By this time Christmas was looming ever nearer, I felt more lonely at that time than I ever felt during the past 8 years, there was a huge hole inside of me, an emptiness which I had never felt before in my life, not even when leaving my mum did I feel like this!

Me and Mellow had a very special relationship as he was my confidante, best friend and family, even today I have never gotten over losing him. I had my beautiful, loving Mellow cremated, the vet practice organised this for me and 2 weeks later I collected his ashes and placed them in a rabbit-shaped urn inside my glass cabinet, next to Melody's urn, so they could be together. I had a heart-shaped pendant made containing some of Mellow's ashes. Since putting it on, I have never taken it off, that way he is always next to my heart.

I bought Edwina, my friend, a similar pendant to mine so that she would remember him too, after all, it was she who brought him into my life and my heart. It was Edwina that I told first about losing him, he and Sky, Edwina's dog were best friends too. Mellow really loved Sky, they had a great relationship.

Due to Mellow being a very special bunny, I made a decision to write his life story and to have it published. This I have done and it is available to buy on Amazon. The book is titled "Mellow's Tale". That way, whoever reads the book will perhaps understand what a special pet and companion he was to me, he was loved very much.

I cannot remember about Christmas that year, the new year arrived, along with my depression. I rang my doctor, who suggested that I contact a counsellor, however as there was a 4-6 month waiting list on the NHS, I had to pay privately for one to help me. She would ring me every week, we would talk things through, it did help me, the month of January just flew by.

We were now in February and I began to look at pet sites online for an older rabbit to offer a good home to. On these sites, it covered budgies and other pets. I managed to contact a budgie breeder around 20 miles away, who told me that his budgies would be ready around the end of March time. I fancied a blue or lilac male one, he said that he would let me know when one became available, so that was okay for me. I did find a lovely site just for rabbits, though most of them were babies. I required an older rabbit, like Mellow. It had to be a Dutch rabbit, as they have such a loving, placid, sweet nature.

I did find one which was around 8 or 9 months old at the time, he was called Shadow. As I still had not gotten over my loss, I asked the young woman who was selling him, if she would mind keeping him for me as I knew that I wanted him and I could offer him a nice, loving home. She agreed not to sell him, so in time, I would have Shadow living with me.

Around the beginning of March that year, news of the Covid-19 pandemic hit the television and radio. At that time, I thought perhaps the budgie breeder had forgotten about me, but towards the end of March and one day before the first Covid lockdown, he offered to travel to me as he had 2 budgies for me to look at. As they had been together from being very young, I felt due to this I could not part them, so I kept them both, a beautiful lilac-coloured budgie whom I named Barley, the other one a beautiful aqua and white coloured budgie whom I named Farley. In time they became best friends.

42

March and April were not good months for me, as my depression really kicked in, also as we were in lockdown, this did not help at all. Around the second week in April, I contacted the rabbit breeder who had been holding onto Shadow for me, hoping that she still had him, which she did.

At that time, my friend Karen was unable to do any more shopping for me, mainly due to the impact of the Covid-19 virus, so I knew that the British government had set up a volunteer service for people to call at your home, to do your weekly shop. I contacted them around the beginning of April, they put me on the waiting list for a volunteer in my area. Around one week later, a gentleman called Steve contacted me to say that he would like to do my shopping for me. At that time, if you had any form of disability, you were classed as vulnerable, which I was. Steve came the following week to collect my list, he was very reliable and competent, which was good and we got on quite well, which was a bonus. So, after knowing Steve for a few weeks, I asked him if he could do me a favour and take me to look at Shadow as he was living on the outskirts of Nottingham. It was a long way to travel, as it was a one-off trip, I offered Steve some money for his petrol, which he did not accept. We arrived at the house and found Shadow in a very small hutch. There were a lot of rabbits there, most were baby ones. As I had already paid for Shadow, no money exchanged hands. I loved him at first sight, knowing that I had done the right thing. He was placed in the pet basket and put in the back of Steve's car with me, so I could talk to Shadow and calm him down as rabbits do not like travelling around.

Since then, I have kept in touch with Shadow's previous owner and we have become good friends. Shadow, like Farley and Harley, was very scared and nervous at first. When I put him into his big cage in the lounge, it was so very different for him, having been living outside in a little hutch, so now he had to adjust to being inside a cage with a person he did not know.

The following months of May, June and July saw me concentrating on Shadow, Farley and Harley, trying to bond with them all, which I did in time. During these months, my depression was bad. I was not having counselling at that time, I was just trying to keep myself as busy as I could. My pets took up a lot of my time as did all my various hobbies which I loved to do. Before I knew it, August was here, it brought hot, sunny days and muggy nights. I would sit outside, sometimes in the evening, or perhaps I would go for a ride on my mobility scooter, just to get some much-needed fresh air. September started warm too, which was nice, by then Shadow, Farley and Harley had settled in, all having different personalities.

43

My two budgies, Farley and Harley really got on with each other. Farley the male budgie was the boss, he was loud. Harley, although a male budgie, was quiet and sweet, he would follow him everywhere around their cage, so they complimented each other. They became very close. In time, I taught them to come onto my hand for seed millet spray and various treats, something Farley still does to this day. Shadow, my bunny, is just such a loving, sweet, placid boy, he likes nothing more than being stroked behind his ears. As he was only 8 months old when I got him, he was a lot younger than Mellow, though he does have a much gentler nature, he is not stubborn, just loving. Harley, the lilac budgie was very loving, sweet and gentle-natured, we really bonded well. Around the second week of September, I did not feel too well in myself, so I spent 4 days in bed to rest, as every time I got up, I felt dizzy, hot, sweaty and just not well at all. This went on for around 2-3 weeks, after which I recovered, I did not go out during this time, though I did manage to look after all my pets as they were my priority.

When October came around, Shadow had begun to get used to his cage, his new home and me of course. I would let him out of his cage once a week to have a run around my bedroom to stretch his legs. Although I was able to take him out of his cage, it was a different story to get him back in again. I found Shadow just too fast for me to catch, so as I had made friends with one of the ladies who worked in the office here, she would always help me. Having rabbits herself, she knew how to handle them and she would catch Shadow for me which I was grateful for.

My birthday as always was quiet again for me, though this year my friend Edwina said that we should go out for lunch at a local golf club, which had a lovely restaurant. We did this, it was good for me to do something different and I enjoyed it.

Once more, the winter beckoned, the nights were drawing in, the days becoming colder with strong winds and rain in between.

November was a wet, rainy, damp month, so I kept myself busy with my sewing, knitting and various other hobbies. Also, I started to write this autobiography, along with another book, these all kept me occupied.

Christmas day was just like any other, I was at home with all my pets, like always. New year 2021, I wondered what was in store for me this year. Little did I know that I would meet a new male friend, whom I would come to think a lot of, perhaps more than he did for me.

44

A Friend For Me

The month of January 2021 was wet and cold, though we had no snowfall, which was a good thing as here we are high up, when it snowed it did snow a lot.

Steve would call each week, to do my shopping, I would often go with him. Towards the end of January or the beginning of February, he told me that he would be going to France at the end of March for 4 months or so as he had a cottage out there, so he would no longer be able to do my weekly shop. He advised me to ring the NHS voluntary helpline to get registered for another volunteer to help me with the shopping call. At that time in February, he took me to have my first Covid-19 injection. I had no side effects from it, I was just pleased to have it done and be covered. I only went out then for appointments and sometimes to Tesco with Steve.

February and March were cold, miserable months. It had been one year since the first lockdown and now I found myself with no one to do my weekly shop. I did contact the NHS volunteer helpline, who put me on a waiting list for someone to go shopping for me. 3 weeks passed and I was going myself to do the shopping, though with my spinal problems, I did find it a lot for me. I decided to ask Lisa who worked in the office on the second floor if she knew of any of the residents in the flats who could help me as most of them had cars. She said that she would ask around, which she did. The following week a nice kindly gentleman called Phil came to see me and offered to do my weekly shopping for me, which was very kind of him.

So, in the third week of April, Phil came to collect my shopping list, and we would have a chat. When he returned with the goods, he would never step inside my flat due to the Covid virus, as at that time most people were wearing face masks anyway. I found Phil very pleasant to talk to, he had a good personality and a sense of humour which I liked, also like me, he too came from Yorkshire. In time, we became friends and I must admit I did look forward to seeing him regularly. I felt that I could talk to him about anything which was great for me. However, I do feel that I became too fond of Phil, I guess it was because I needed him, though as time went on, I started to have romantic feelings towards him. He told me that he was separated from his wife, who did not live in the area. He never saw anything of her, I was led to believe that they lived separate lives. In time, I found out that Phil was very deep and would not tell me much about his wife, which in a way I was glad about.

My favourite month was here at last, May, we had some lovely May sunshine and a few warmer days. My depression had now lifted, as I was feeling very confident about the months ahead, it was then that I started to write my very first book, "Mellow's Tale".

In June, we had a few weeks of nice sunshine, taken over by rain showers. My rabbit was becoming more tame with me, as were my two lovely sweet budgies, Farley and Harley. June was a lovely, sunny month. Phil came every week and we would have a chat, a laugh too, with a little flirting too on both sides, quite light-hearted. At that time, I was classed as vulnerable, I only went out once a day on my mobility scooter. Phil was the only person I saw each week. The summer this year was temperamental, it could be raining one day, and sunny the next, so you never knew what to wear. I had booked two small breaks away, which were cancelled due to the Covid-19 pandemic. I rather thought this would happen.

When August arrived, the beginning of the month was quite warm, then towards the end of August we had some cool winds with more rain to follow. In the second week of September, Phil came to see me, he told me that unfortunately, he could no longer do my shopping as he was moving back to Skegness to the flat his wife had lived in as she had passed away in August. As you can imagine, I was a little upset about him moving back to Skegness.

He told me that he was moving in 10 days, so he suggested that he would ask one of his neighbours if they could help me out to do the shopping. Phil did ask his neighbour, who told him that he would not be able to do this for me. As I thought a lot about Phil, he meant so much to me, I was very disappointed that I would not be seeing him again, but told him that I would give him a ring sometime, which I did around the beginning of October. As we chatted, I felt that he seemed different somehow; he was aloof and not as jolly and happy in himself as he was when he lived in the flat.

I suggested that perhaps one of my friends could drive me over to Skegness for the day and then we could meet up for a coffee or lunch even. He was quite pleased about this at the time. However, after the phone call, I watched the evening news which said that Skegness was rather busy at that time. This put me off going, due to Covid, so I decided to ring him the next day to let him know that I did not feel it was safe for me to go to Skegness at that particular time because of the Covid virus. Phil answered the phone on the second ring and as I explained that he became very abrupt, raising his voice with me, then he put the phone down on me, which I thought was very rude of him; all because I was unable to visit him!

The next day I received a text message from Phil which was not nice at all, quite hurtful in fact, he had shown his true colours to me. So, although I was hurt and upset about this, thinking about things, I felt that this was for the best anyway, though I did have the last word, as I replied to him with a text of my own telling him just exactly what I thought of him. So, that was the end of our friendship. Looking back, I really believe he did me a favour.

I had another quiet birthday in October, by that time the weather had turned foggy, damp and cold most days and winter was on the way once again. At that time of year, most people's thoughts turned to Christmas, gifts, trees, snow etc. As we still had Covid with us, it would be a lonely Christmas for a lot of people who lived on their own and who were unable to gather with their families to celebrate the season. I spent November on my own, with my pets, though by this time, I had contacted a care firm, for a carer to call once a fortnight to do my shopping for me, so at least I had some help with this task.

November flew by, as did December; we had no snow, and the carer came to me around Christmas time. It was nice to be able to chat with someone again as it was not the weather for me to go out for a ride on my mobility scooter. I occupied myself with all my hobbies and caring for my pets, I always had something to do which was good.

2022 now beckoned, I just hoped that this new year we would all be able to get back to some sort of normality and be able to get together once again and start to get on with our lives, without having to worry too much about Covid.

45

January 2022 came around with thoughts of New Year resolutions. The only thing I really wanted to do this year was to finish my story, my own autobiography. The way it was going this would be achieved perhaps by November time. I felt very positive about this year, which was good for me. After the last year, with the 2 sad losses which I suffered and how they really affected me mentally with my depression and everything. I decided that this year was going to be my year and up to now it has been.

I always feel that January is too long a month and this year was no exception. By February, some of the little buds were showing above the soil around my small patio area, in their plant pots, spring would be soon here. I like to see all the spring flowers, spring is such a wonderful time of year. February was cold, though we did have a few much-needed frosts along the way. By the second week of March, the days seemed to be getting lighter and longer.

Easter would fall late this year; I did not mind as I did nothing for Easter anyway. I did manage to go for an interview at the local air ambulance charity shop to become a volunteer, and I would start there the next week, the second week of April. I had been working there only 3 weeks when after handling the clothes, the very next day I felt very poorly in myself. I had no energy, I was using the toilet frequently. I ended up being in bed for 5 days. I could not keep anything down, all I could manage to do was to care for my pets, feeding them and cleaning them out, when I could, nothing more, as I felt so dizzy being up, I had to go back to bed and rest.

I did have the carers coming in to do the shopping which was a help. I spoke to my local pharmacist who told me that it was a sickness bug, he did advise me to drink plenty of water and to rest up, which I did. After resting for 5-6 days, when I was able to get up, I felt so weak in myself, lethargic and tired, physically, it really did take it out of me, so much so that it took me around 5 weeks to be fully better. By that time, it was near to my holiday, which I had booked to go to Cromer in Norfolk. I had booked the break away in April but sadly, this had to be cancelled as I was not well enough to travel.

The month of March was quite nice; we had some mild, dry days at the beginning. I had found a nice group in town by then which met on a Wednesday; it was a social group for people like me who suffered from depression and anxiety, where we could meet socially to have a chat and a cuppa. I had been a few times in March, having made a nice new friend there called Susie. She came to pick me up from home the first Wednesday of May to take me to the group, which was kind of her and so began another chapter of my life as in time, both me and Susie became quite close, good friends. We just really get on, which is good as she is such a kind, sweet, caring, thoughtful person.

46

New Friends For Me

I really look forward to going to the group as I always feel much better and calmer in myself afterwards. My holiday to Cromer soon came around. I was travelling by coach and staying in a hotel for 5 days. Having not been to Cromer in a little while, I was looking forward to this break away, but mainly looking forward to meeting up with my friend, Lynn, who used to be my neighbour. She had moved to Norfolk to be nearer to her family who lived near Norwich. We arrived at the hotel late afternoon, the weather was warm and dry and the hotel was lovely. I went down for the evening meal after having a rest, and I managed to speak to some of the people from the coach.

That night, I tried my best to sleep, being somewhere new it was always hard for me. The next day around 11 a.m, Lynn came to the hotel. It was really great to see her again; we went to a local garden centre, and then she took me back to her place. Her house was very nice. I returned to the hotel in time for dinner, having had a lovely day with Lynn.

The next day we all went on the coach to Wells and then on to Sheringham which I had never visited before. It was a long day out for me, so after dinner, I decided to have an early night, which I did. Lynn came for me the next day, we went to another garden centre where we had a look around and stopped for lunch, arriving back at the hotel around five o'clock. The following day was our leaving day, we stopped off at King's Lynn for a few hours. I really did enjoy my break away, the highlight for me was seeing my friend, Lynn, as we both had a lot in common and liked similar things.

I arrived home feeling tired, having enjoyed my Norfolk break, although I was looking forward to seeing my pets again. However, I did not feel too good the next day as I had brought home a cold with me from Norfolk. I did not go to my group the following week, Edwina came to give me my acupuncture on that day, which was great as I needed it.

The following week after my treatment, I rang her, she told me that her lovely dog, Sky, who I had known and loved for 9 years had had to be put to sleep as he was just too poorly in himself. Well as you can imagine, she was very upset and distressed about this, as was I.

Then June came around before I knew it and I made my mind up not to have any more breaks away in the year, only perhaps to go and stay with my friend Lynn in September time as it was her 60th birthday, I could take her gifts. I had known my friend Edwina and her dog Sky for over 9 years. I thought about having Sky painted by an artist, so I looked online and found a nice lady from Derbyshire who was able to paint Sky; that way my friend would always have him with her.

47

Edwina sent the painter a photograph of Sky to go by. I rang her up to tell her that I would like a painting done of him too, which she did, and both paintings are lovely. My painting hangs on my lounge wall so that way Sky is always with me as well.

It was now the end of June; we had a lot of rain, not much sunshine though, the ground and grass were very dry as were my raised flower beds, also pot plants. July now beckoned, it was a little warmer at the start, however, we still had a few showers so I was unable to sit out on my patio area, to get some much-needed fresh air. I still attended my group on a Wednesday though most Wednesdays were a wash-out with all the rainfall. July would be another wet, rainy but mild month. It was mild at least at the start, then around the 12th of the month it began to become quite hot and we had hot, muggy days with lots of sunshine. It really did get hot most days of the month and on the 19th of July, we had the hottest day of the year. All I could do was stay indoors and get cool under my electric fan; it was really too hot for me to go out. However, on saying that, I decided to paint all my raised flower beds on my patio area. I would do this at nighttime as it was a lot cooler then to paint.

The rest of July was much the same. I did not have any coach breaks booked for July, which was good as I felt that it would be too much for me to travel in the heat. I still went to my social group, which I always enjoyed, it meant that I was able to see some of my friends there, and in particular, Susie. August came around and with it more of the same hot, dry, muggy weather. I went on a train for the first time in 6 years to a small market town to have a look around at the shops. I stopped at a café there to have some lunch, which was nice.

I decided to buy some new blinds for my lounge as I had had them for over 8 years, I fancied a change of colour and style. The man came to measure up for them, it would take six weeks before they would be fitted.

I looked at the coach holiday brochures and found one which looked interesting, it was to go to Bristol to see the hot air balloons and to stay in a hotel in the town. It was a 2-night, 3-day break which was nice. By this time, it was now 2 weeks before my break away, the date being the 12th of August. I was really looking forward to this different kind of trip. I was to catch the coach in Loughborough, travelling there by taxi. However, what I did not know at the time was just what a big disappointment the whole break would be for me. I was very excited about this trip as I had always wanted to see some hot air balloons. I boarded the coach in Loughborough, not knowing then what was in store for all of us on the coach.

48
Holiday Disaster

We all set off down to Bristol, making it in good time to Bath, where we stopped off for a few hours. I had to look around the shops, it was a beautiful but very hot, sunny day again, so I stopped for a cup of tea and a nice piece of cake in a quaint little café. I really enjoyed visiting Bath, it is such a good, interesting town, lots to see and do. Then we all boarded the coach again, arriving at the hotel at 5 o'clock. I was glad to get to my room, looking forward to my dinner, though what I did not realise was that dinner was not included as it was on a bed and breakfast basis. The hotel did provide meals which you had to pay separately for. So, as there was a nice restaurant in the hotel, I had a meal, though only for one night as the price of the meals was quite expensive. This was disappointing for me as the full cost of the holiday was not cheap.

I could not sleep that night, waking up to a hot, dry, sunny day, I went down for my breakfast which was self-service, like a lot of hotels were. We left the hotel around ten in the morning to travel to the hot air balloon festival. However, the coach driver could not locate the venue or indeed where he could park his coach. When we did eventually arrive at the coach park, the driver informed us that we all had to walk to the event which was over a motorway and 1½ miles away, so I asked him to ring for a taxi as I was unable to walk that far, and I did not feel safe crossing over a main road. The taxi driver arrived around 20 minutes later. I arrived at the venue and was informed that the hot air balloons had set off early in the morning so there were no balloons for anyone to see.

As there were only a few stalls and cafes, I just could not imagine staying there very long as there was nothing to see and do, so as I had befriended a lady on the coach, after 2 hours we decided we had had enough. We rang for a taxi to take us back to the coach park, which we did, both feeling very despondent and disappointed indeed. The coach driver approached us both, we told him just how disappointed and upset we were to not see the hot air balloons and he suggested that as there were a few of us, he would take us back to the hotel. We arrived back around 3 p.m., all feeling let down and despondent.

That evening, I decided to walk to a pizza place, which was 2 minutes away from the hotel. I had a lovely meal that night, getting back to the hotel at about 10 o'clock, I went straight up to my room and packed my case, as we were leaving for home the next day. I would be glad to get home as the whole break had been a disappointment to me in so many ways. I would be writing a letter of complaint to the coach holiday company, which I did.

49

My Pets

As one of my neighbours had been looking after my pets for me whilst away, I just hoped that she had done a good job. But when I returned home around seven o'clock, tired from travelling, well what greeted me was not good at all, as 2 of my danio fish were dead, both my pets were scared of me, also my front door would not lock properly, so after an awful holiday I came home to this. It would be one break away I will remember but for all the wrong reasons!

The rest of August was very hot and dry, so hot we went into a drought. It had not rained for so many days, everything looked parched and dry. By the end of the month, we had been advised not to use water hoses and to use water wisely, which I did anyway. I really like the month of September, so I thought that it would be a good idea to go to see my friend Lynn who lived in Norfolk as I would travel by train. I had arranged for some help with my luggage and this turned out to be a much better break away for me. I stayed with Lynn for 3 days, the train being quite busy, though I did enjoy it, and it was great for me to see Lynn again. Whilst there, we visited various places in north Norfolk and 2 garden centres. Before I knew it, it was time for me to return home, this was a relaxing break for both of us as Lynn worked so hard, being a carer in a nursing home.

Lynn set me to the train station on the last day. I was on my way home again, only this time I had arranged for my friend Edwina to take care of all my pets, so I knew that they would be okay. I really enjoyed my Norfolk break away, looking forward to perhaps seeing Lynn again next year. September was a nice warm month, right through. It would be my birthday again soon; this year has just flown by as have the past 2 years since Covid 19 has been with us all.

I have never liked the month of October, as I have too many sad memories of past events so I really was not very excited about my birthday. My birthday for me would just be another day, one I would spend on my own, like I usually did, only this year I would not be on my own. October arrived and all my sad memories returned, especially about my dear brother who lost his life at sea on a trawler. I just cannot believe that it was 44 years ago. I will never, ever forget him and all the sadness that followed. The whole family split up, I do know my mum would always remind me of that very sad, distressing time in our lives.

This year October was quite mild to start. I would get to know my new friend Susie more. We were and are very much alike in our natures anyway, which is nice. Around the second week of October, my budgie, Farley, lost his voice. For some reason, this was unlike him, as Farley is very vocal, so I took him to the avian vet to be checked over and for some advice as to why this was. He thought that it could be seasonal, with the days becoming darker, hence less light, so he suggested that I buy an avian UV lamp. As I had one already at home, I made it up and placed Farley under it, within a few days his voice returned, this was great I thought, the lamp seemed to be helping him.

Then, before I knew it my birthday was upon me. As I had been so worried and stressed about Farley, I had a few days in which I did not feel well at all, one of those days was on my birthday. My friend Susie rang me that day to say that she and her boyfriend would be coming to see me, as she had a card and a present for me. They arrived one hour later, it was so good to see her again, we had a long chat, and a catch up on news, and other things. It was good of her to call, at least I was not on my own this year. It was nice for me to have some company; they stayed for about an hour and left. Susie really made my birthday this year certainly more pleasant than it would have been otherwise. I received lots of cards, flowers and gifts, all in all, I really had a lovely day.

That week I went along to my group, Susie was there as were quite a few of the regulars. I started a small painting that day which would be finished the following week. I had planned to go on the bus to Loughborough and on the train to Stamford, 2 trips I have not done as of yet. The end of October and Halloween were in sight by this time, also bonfire night was not far off in November. Both these things I do nothing for, I never have, only when I was a child both me and my sister were given sparklers to play with. Mum would supervise us as regards Halloween, neither me or my sister would go trick or treating as Mum did not allow it.

I rang a woman at that time who was a manager of one of the charity shops in town as I had made a friend of her earlier in the year. We had a long talk, and I mentioned that I enjoyed looking around garden centres and she suggested that on the 1st of November, we would visit one and have some lunch whilst there. On the 1st of November, she came to collect me and we went off to the garden centre. We had a really nice time there, lunch was enjoyable as I never go out for lunch, and this made a change for me, something different. She enjoyed our trip there as much as I did, it was just great for me to get out and see new places. The only drawback that day was the rain; we had lots of it. November up to now has been a very wet month indeed.

50

Me and My Pets

November always seemed a short month to me, at least at the start it was mild, we just had to put up with all the rainy weather. I went to my group that week, also my English class, though I was very concerned about my budgie Farley once more, as you know when something is not right with your pet. This time he started to have seizures, they were now and again at first, then within a week they increased to every day he was having one. It was most upsetting for me to see him like that. I monitored him at the beginning, then as he seemed to be becoming worse with the seizures, I had no choice but to ring the vet for their advice.

The vet required to see Farley, so I arranged a taxi to take us both to the PDSA hospital as the avian vet was unable to see him, being fully booked at the time. The next evening I took Farley to the PDSA hospital; the vet looked at him and told me that she thought he had an infection, she prescribed a medicine which I had to give him via a syringe into his mouth. As it was difficult for me to do this on my own, my friend helped me and after one week, he seemed a lot better in himself. Then for some reason, he started once again with the seizures. I rang the avian vet who had an appointment for Farley the next day. So we went to see the vet who examined Farley and said that he thought he had been poisoned by either a metal toy from his cage or even the metal bars in his cage.

He told me that he would like to monitor Farley for 2-3 days to see if he had any seizures, so it meant that little Farley had to stay in the vet hospital for 3 days. During this time, I really did miss him as it seemed so quiet at home.

On the fourth day, I managed to speak to the vet, who told me that whilst there, Farley had no seizures. I asked him what he thought could have been the cause. He stated that it could have been his UV avian lamp or the extra liquid calcium I had been giving him. He told me that Farley could come home and so I arranged for a taxi to take me to the pet hospital as Farley was coming home at last!

I was really worried about my Farley as I was so stressed and anxious during this time, I had lost 6lbs in weight, also my hair seemed to be a lot thinner; all this I put down to stress and worry as Farley had been so poorly with the seizures. Since being home 2 weeks, I have not put him under the UV lamp or given him any liquid calcium supplement and he has been just fine, back to his own self, chirping, tweeting, cute little bird that he is, he really is a character.

Now it has turned cold, winter is definitely here with Christmas not far off too. Recently, I have been supporting my friend Susie as she has not been too good in herself. I text her most days and also my friend Edwina. It seems that nearly everyone I know is not well with either a cold, flu or even Covid. Up to now, I have kept quite well, though I do feel that we are due some snow soon as it has been very cold in the day and also at night.

I had an appointment at the start of this week to see my doctor who was pleased with me. He said that I was very positive about the future, which despite everything that has occurred this year and the worrying time ahead for everyone, I guess that I am positive. I am a totally different person from nearly 11 years ago. I have changed for the better of course, as I now look ahead, not back at the past times and memories which went before. No good comes of that, I do not want to think of all the sadness in my past. I feel that once again this year is going to be my year, who knows just what is in store for me?

One thing I do know though is I will continue to grow, to become wiser, to learn to meet new and interesting people, to make new friends, to travel, to be with old friends and to give, as I am a very giving person, to care possibly even to love and find true love one day. All these things are possible and attainable, you just have to reach out for them.

I am happy, very happy with this new life I have made for myself and I am so looking forward to the next chapter of my life and of course writing my next book, which should be very interesting. So, as I look ahead to whatever next year will bring my way, I would like to thank Jehovah my God for all his support and guidance throughout my whole life, all my friends for their friendship, support and care, for all my pets, past and present who have given me unconditional love, and brought me so much joy and happiness over the years. I have really loved looking after them, being so grateful for all their company and for being with me.

So, as this book is finally brought to an end, I look back over my life, throughout the many years and look forward with confidence to the years to come, whatever will be will be.

Available worldwide from Amazon

Michael Terence Publishing

www.mtp.agency

mtp.agency

@mtp_agency

Printed in Great Britain
by Amazon

39306639R00116